THE PEACE APPROACH TO VIOLENCE PREVENTION

A Guide for Administrators and Teachers

Kimberly M. Williams

A SCARECROWEDUCATION BOOK

The Scarecrow Press, Inc.
Lanham, Maryland, and Oxford
2003

A SCARECROWEDUCATION BOOK

Published in the United States of America
by Scarecrow Press, Inc.
A Member of the Rowman & Littlefield Publishing Group
4501 Forbes Boulevard, Suite 200, Lanham, Maryland 20706
www.scarecroweducation.com

PO Box 317
Oxford
OX2 9RU, UK

British Library Cataloguing in Publication Information Available

Library of Congress Cataloging-in-Publication Data
Williams, Kimberly M., 1968–
  The PEACE approach to violence prevention: a guide for administrators and
teachers / Kimberly M. Williams.
     p. cm.
"A ScarecrowEducation book."
Includes bibliographical references.
  ISBN 0-8108-4623-3 (pbk. : alk. paper)
  1. School violence—United States—Prevention. 2. Behavior modification.
I. Title.
LB3013.32 .W55 2003
371.7'82'0973—dc21
                                                                    2002013870

∞™ The paper used in this publication meets the minimum requirements of
American National Standard for Information Sciences—Permanence of Paper
for Printed Library Materials, ANSI/NISO Z39.48-1992.
Manufactured in the United States of America.

For Whitney.
May you and the rest of the world's children always
learn in peaceful schools.

CONTENTS

ACKNOWLEDGMENTS

First and foremost, I would like to acknowledge and thank my family for their love and support throughout the creation of this book and without whom this book would not have been created.

Many projects at many schools (the names have been changed to preserve anonymity) have culminated in the writing of this book. I would like to thank all of the administrators, parents, teachers, staff, and students who worked with me on gathering data for this project. Also, thank you to my colleagues and funding agencies. Some of the funding for the research described in this book was made available from the Hamilton Fish National Institute on School and Community Violence. The funding was from Grant No. 97-MU-FX-KO12 (S-1) from the Office of Juvenile Justice and Delinquency Prevention, Office of Justice Programs, U.S. Department of Justice.

In addition, some funding was made available from Contact, Inc. of Syracuse, New York. Points of view or opinions in this book are those of the author and do not necessarily represent those of the U.S. Department of Justice or Contact, Inc.

INTRODUCTION

We need a plan for dealing with violence in schools, yet one plan will not make sense for all schools and all people within schools. Not all people define violence the same way. Not all schools have the same violence problems. Not all programs are created equal. Not all components work in every environment. The PEACE approach outlined in this book is designed to address the many definitions of violence as well as the differences that exist among individuals and schools. As schools are mandated to address the problems of violence in a systematic way, the PEACE approach offers a framework that can make sense within any school environment. Teachers and administrators alike can start the process—even before they are certified or hired.

The PEACE approach includes the following steps:

Personalize the experience of violence. Begin with your own perspectives and definitions of violence and what counts as violent. These personal experiences are critical in shaping our understanding of violence and what we notice about it. This first step helps us understand our personal biases and the importance of our personal experiences.

Examine experiences of students in the school. After exploring their own perspectives on violence, teachers, administrators, researchers, and others are invited to explore how students in their particular school make sense of violence. What acts do they notice? What do they take for granted? Through a series of possible strategies (interviews, observations, formal and informal surveys, and focus groups), we need to gain a picture of what concerns students most regarding issues of violence.

Advocate for students based on their needs. Once the needs are identified, the next step is to advocate for these needs. Part of advocacy includes educating oneself about the components of programs with demonstrated success and determining which components will best suit the needs of students.

Choose and implement program components. With the decision makers in the school, choose and implement program components that seem to be most appropriate, given the needs of your students. Examples of particular programs and components are given using two different case studies.

Evaluate effectiveness. Finally, critically important but often left out, is evaluating how effective the intervention is. Was violent behavior less frequent? Do students feel safer? Are they more aware of the impact of cruel treatment? In a nutshell, were the identified needs met? Two examples of evaluations of the interventions implemented at the case study sites are described.

This book provides a step-by-step approach to understanding and dealing with violence in schools, using examples from two extremely different case studies using this approach. One school was an alternative school for students who had been caught with a weapon in school (pseudonym WANTS—Weapons Are Not the Solution). The other was an affluent suburban middle school (pseudonym Deerfield). These examples will demonstrate the need for the PEACE strategy when schools attempt to address school violence or as schools of education prepare future teachers to address the needs of future students. There is no one-size-fits-all solution to school violence. This framework allows educators to tailor programs that will work for them, given the needs of their students.

①

STEP I OF THE PEACE
APPROACH: PERSONALIZE

WHY PERSONALIZE THE EXPERIENCE

How Does One Start?

As educators, we need to analyze our own personal definitions of violence. What comes to mind immediately when you hear the word *violence*? What do we consider violent? What have our personal experiences been with violence? What violent acts do we notice? What acts do we find most problematic? We need to acknowledge what we consider violent because this will shape what we notice—and what we fail to notice—among our students. Our own experiences shape our definitions. Our definitions shape our biases. Our biases affect the way we act and react in attempting to reduce violence in our schools. We must start with ourselves first, then seek to find out about the experiences of our students and how they define violence (described in the next chapter).

Definitions of Violence

Those studying violence do not have an agreed-upon definition of violence, let alone school violence. You will find that there are many different perspectives—your own included. Some definitions are as follows:

- "Violence is the act of purposefully hurting someone" according to the definition put forth by the American Psychological Association (Warning Signs 1999, 1). The definition is elegant in its simplicity. In this definition, you may notice the term *purposeful*, which covers the issue of intent. One intends to cause hurt—and it is not clear if it is physical or emotional hurt or both. Also, "someone" is hurt—it is not completely clear if it must be another person or if it can be oneself, as in the case of self-mutilation or suicide.
- Merriam-Webster's Collegiate Dictionary defines violence as the following:

1a: exertion of physical force so as to injure or abuse (as in effecting illegal entry into a house) b: an instance of violent treatment or procedure 2: injury by or as if by distortion, infringement, or profanation: OUTRAGE 3a: intense, turbulent, or furious and often destructive action or force <the *violence* of the storm> b: vehement feeling or expression: FERVOR; *also*: an instance of such action or feeling c: a clashing or jarring quality: DISCORDANCE
4: undue alteration (as of wording or sense in editing a text). (Definition available at www.m-w.com/cgi-bin/dictionary?book=Dictionary&va= violence.)

This kind of focus on physical violence has tended to be the cause of our attention, while other forms of verbal harm are often overlooked.

- The Centers for Disease Control defines violence as "the threatened or actual use of physical force or power against another person, against oneself, or against a group or community which results in or has a high likelihood of resulting in injury, death, or deprivation" (Centers for Disease Control 2001, 1). This definition has the threat of violence included as well as the actual act of violence and directly refers to another person, self, or community. Although verbal assault is not spelled out exactly, the idea of "deprivation" is. Although not explicitly stated, this definition could include depriving people from resources such as money, power, or an appropriate education as violence.

- The Johnson Institute/Hazelden defines violence as occurring "whenever anyone inflicts or threatens to inflict physical or emotional injury or discomfort upon another person's body, feelings, or possessions" (Remboldt 1994, 1). This definition includes "possessions." Teachers and administrators are much more likely to fall victim to theft than forms of physical violence, and yet theft or damaging one's property (car, home, etc.) is often left out of our definitions of violence.

- MacDonald attempted to come up with a comprehensive definition of school violence based on her work in schools (1998, 19): "School violence represents those actual or threatened behaviors or actions that are symptomatic of an unfulfilled need (e.g., to belong, have power, seek approval), expressed in the form of sexual, emotional, or physical harm, that has a deleterious effect on establishing and maintaining a safe and caring school climate." MacDonald tries with this definition to also describe some of the root causes of school violence—something rarely attempted in definitions. Also, she spells out "sexual" as well as "emotional" harm, as well as "actual" or "threatened" behavior.

- Finally, peace activist, author, and educator Johan Galtung (1969, 168) offered a comprehensive definition of violence that helped provide a framework for this project in his article "Violence, Peace, and Peace Research." He defines peace as the "absence of violence." He rejects a narrow definition of violence that focuses on intended physical or psychological harm and instead writes, "Let us say that violence is present when human beings are being so influenced so that their actual somatic (physical) and mental realizations are below their potential realizations." He believes his definition will likely "lead to more problems than it solves." For Galtung, poverty is violence, as is deprivation. Students attending underfunded schools, in Galtung's view, would be victims of violence.

Definitions vary in their wording and focus but there are some commonalities, such as the focus on harm. Schools, school boards, national organizations, and others have tried to come to a consensus on a working definition for violence so that they can speak the same language and have some agreement and focus.

The work of personalizing violence is challenging. We must do some soul searching and think about what we truly believe about violence. There is a lot of violence tolerated and even promoted every day within American culture. Some sports, video games, popular media (television, radio, film, etc.) are filled with violent images. We have come to accept fighting in self-defense as nearly always acceptable if someone is being victimized, yet the line between victim and perpetrator can sometimes be blurry. Children who are perpetrators are nearly always victims someplace else in their lives; how can we address the needs of a child who is a perpetrator and a victim? How do we react to victimization versus perpetration? Our political actions concerning the death penalty and fighting wars before exploring all options of diplomacy show young people that violence can be justified. Teachers and administrators who publicly humiliate and degrade children to get them to comply with their rules suggest to children that bullying can achieve desired results. We need to examine our own behaviors as well as the actions we support in our society as we begin this work of personalizing violence.

ACTIVITY AND DISCUSSION

Questions for Discussion

Do you believe, as Galtung does, that mere deprivation or poverty is violence? Is your definition as simple and concrete as the one offered by the American Psychological Association? Do these definitions help you or make the issue more complex? Defining violence is complex. You, your colleagues, your students, their parents, and others may all have very different perspectives and experiences and, therefore, definitions. Because our definitions shape our approaches to the problem of school violence, we need to understand our own definitions and those of others.

The definition needs to start with our own personal views of what constitutes violence and then move on to how those in our school define violence.

Activity

In groups, this can be done on a board or newsprint, writing responses with markers and asking those in the group to use single words to summarize what they think is violent, and come up and circle those words that they have personally experienced. This can also be done as an individual journal-writing activity.

Consider the following questions:

- What do you consider violent?
- What words come to mind when you hear the word *violence*?
- What have your personal experiences been with violence, both in and out of school?
- What violent acts do you notice?
- What acts do you find most problematic?
- Do you find any acts of violence acceptable? When and why?
- If done as a group activity, what commonalities do you notice? What is left out? What seems controversial?

2

STEP 2 OF THE PEACE
APPROACH: EXAMINE

Now that you and your colleagues have a sense of your own perspectives of violence, it is important to get a better sense of students' perspectives of violence in their lives. The second step in the PEACE plan is to examine the experiences of students regarding violence. How do your students make sense of violence? What do they define as problematic types of violence? What are they afraid of in terms of violence? What acts do they consider most violent and dangerous to themselves? What acts do they see on a regular basis? What behaviors do they think need to be addressed? What acts go unnoticed, or what behaviors associated with violence do they accept as a part of going to school? Students will tell you a great deal and you can learn a lot from listening and observing. After addressing your own biases regarding violence, you are in a better position to listen to and observe your students' experiences with respect to school violence.

There are informal and more formal ways to gather information about student perspectives. The informal strategies include observations, informal surveys, focus groups or discussions with students about violence, journal writing, and interviews. Formal strategies include use of formal surveys and behavioral tests, identification of risk factors, and identification of warning signs for acting-out and depressive behaviors.

Whether using informal or formal strategies, guaranteeing anonymity as much as possible to students is essential when gathering information about what kinds of violence students experience and find most problematic.

It is also essential that, as teachers and administrators examining issues of violence in your school, you pay particular attention to the kinds of behaviors that students often underreport—bullying, relational aggression, and relationship violence. These three underreported forms of violence are typically accepted by children and are described toward the end of this chapter.

EXAMINING YOUR STUDENTS' EXPERIENCES AND PERCEPTIONS

The following are informal strategies you can use to examine your students' needs:

- Observation (classrooms, hallways, cafeteria, and "hot spots" where violence is most common)
- Focus groups (small groups of students with open-ended questions)
- Journal-writing activities around themes of violence
- Interviews (one on one with students or other school staff)
- Informal, teacher-made surveys (written survey questions including open-ended and Likert-type questions)

Informal strategies are particularly useful for educators to get a better understanding of students' perceptions of violence, what they consider most problematic, what they are most afraid of, what they report, and what they fail to report. Teachers or administrators tend to be very close to students and have a very good sense of what happens in school. However, digging deeper using informal strategies might yield some surprising results—even for teachers or administrators who are very close to and feel they understand where students are coming from related to many issues, including school violence.

Observation

Observation is a popular technique of researchers and evaluators. When used formally, researchers act as observers in a particular setting under investigation. Observers can range from being complete participants in the setting (as is the case with teacher-action research when teachers conduct observation of their own classrooms) to non-participants (silently taking notes without engaging participants; in extreme cases, the participant observes behind one-way glass). Observers take field notes and look for common themes or categories that emerge from their observations and notes. Educators use this technique to gather more information about students' perspectives and experiences.

Teachers or administrators often overhear student conversations about fights. They also often know where the "hot spots" are in the school where much violence occurs (cafeteria, certain darker or under-supervised areas of the school, etc.). You can be an observer in these hot spots and jot down notes to yourself about what you see there. Of course, your mere presence will likely change the behavior, so perhaps you will need to be discreet at first. In addition, purposeful observation within your own classroom—taking notes about student behavior problems (what, where, when, and whom)—will prove to be useful information in planning for your own classroom. Administrators can keep track of problem-behavior student referrals with which they must deal. I worked with an elementary principal at Deerfield who kept a journal of students who were referred, and why and when the referrals were made. She noticed trends—certain students, certain times of day, and certain times of year. She also identified those with chronic behavior problems. This information helped determine what kinds of programs and services were needed for those students.

Focus Groups and Interviews

Focus groups with small groups of students help to gain insight into student perspectives. Focus groups are small groups who are asked a variety of questions by a facilitator, and notes are taken. Sometimes discussions are audiotaped or even videotaped and transcribed; sometimes there is a note taker present during the session. The length and structure of focus groups can vary depending on their purpose. For example, if you want to ask a group of honor students about their perceptions of violence, you can involve groups of six to eight students who meet the stated criteria. This is helpful if you craft questions specific to a group of students (How did you choose to become involved with a gang? Are honor students picked on for doing well in school? In what ways are athletes treated differently in school?). You might want to create more heterogeneous groups and ask a variety of questions that require a variety of responses (e.g., Are students treated cruelly in school? In what ways? What groups of students? What do students do to stay safe?). Whether heterogeneous or homogeneous groups, focus groups allow you to ask open-ended questions and have students respond to you and to each other. You can conduct these as their teacher or administrator, but recognize that because of your position of power, students may not be completely honest with you, and may tell you what they think you want to hear. If you have developed a relationship of trust, students may share openly with you. Enlisting the help of an outside evaluator can sometimes help with focus groups.

At Deerfield, for example, student focus groups yielded a lot of information about the nature of teasing and issues of popularity for middle school students. Students revealed that one of the most significant predictors of popularity was how fast one could run the mile. I asked students how they knew how fast each one could run the mile. They replied that students were timed in the mile early in the year, and that students who were very athletic and ran very fast were among the more popular. Those who were overweight, sickly, or out of shape and could not run as fast were teased more often. This simple activity of having students run the mile and shouting out their times was something that could be changed to prevent this kind of teasing. However, teachers and administrators were unaware of this behavior until it was revealed consistently during focus groups.

You may also elect to interview students in a one-on-one situation if you feel this will allow students to speak candidly with you about their fears and the violence they experience in their lives. Interviews may be very structured with a list of somewhat close-ended questions (Do children hit each other on the bus?) or very unstructured with one or two open-ended questions (Tell me how students treat each other on the bus.). As is the case with interviews, bringing in an outside evaluator is sometimes helpful in designing and conducting interviews.

Journal Writing

Students and others are sometimes willing to share more private thoughts and fears about school violence, gangs, drugs, and other concerns in private writing assignments such as journal-writing activities. These can be crafted to elicit the kinds of information about school violence that you seek. Such questions as "What do you do when you're with your friends outside of school?" or "Describe some situations that have made you afraid in school" lead children to write about their more private feelings—especially if they are guaranteed confidentiality and the teacher has an established record of trust. Teachers have been shocked at what students write during these activities.

In Williams (1998), students were asked to keep a journal about their drug-using experiences. With great candor, students revealed illicit behaviors around their drug-using activities. When administrators read these reports, published with pseudonyms to protect informants' anonymity, they remarked that they were truly surprised and dismayed to learn of the culture of drug use on campus. This silent subculture of drug use often exists outside adult notice. The same is true of violence problems in schools. Therefore, providing a safe alternative for students to write about their experiences and fears can yield some powerful results.

A note of caution about journal writing: sometimes children with low literacy skills may resist the task of writing candidly about their experiences with violence. These are often the same children whose experiences we want to share. Allowing options such as tape recording, videotaping, peer interviews, or even interviews with the teacher (if there is a relationship of trust) will often yield equally powerful results.

Informal or Teacher-Made Surveys

If you have particular behaviors that you suspect are problematic or have particular questions you would like to ask students, you can collaborate with your colleagues to craft informal questionnaires or surveys.

If you are starting from scratch, you may want to create open-ended types of survey questions such as:

- What are you most afraid of at school?
- What kinds of things are most likely to lead students to fight?
- Where are the places to avoid in school because they are unsafe?

These questions give you more information and a place to start. You can look through students' responses and examine them for common themes, categories, or ideas.

Forced-Choice or Likert-Style Questions

If you have some idea of what specific behaviors you would like to know more about, forced-choice or Likert-style questions can be helpful. Using a four- or five-point scale, Likert-style questions ask students to rate an issue in its importance or how often something happens. For example, if you would like to know specifically about students' involvement in gangs, you could ask questions such as "I think gangs are a problem at this school" and provide answers such as "strongly agree," "agree," "disagree," or "strongly disagree." Or "Students say mean things to me" and provide the choices of "often," "sometimes," and "never." If you think bus behavior is problematic, you can ask about that. "I am afraid to ride the bus" with "yes" or "no" (to find out if students are afraid to ride the bus), or you might use "sometimes," "often," or "never" as responses if you would like a better idea of how often a student is afraid to ride the bus.

Likert-style questions often have four or five levels and ask students to rate items to get a wider range of responses, such as the following:

I am afraid to ride the bus to school.

1. Strongly disagree
2. Disagree
3. Undecided
4. Agree
5. Strongly agree

You may want to choose a four-point scale if you want to force a choice and not allow for a "neutral" or "undecided" response, such as:
I feel safe at school.

1 = Strongly agree
2 = Agree
3 = Disagree
4 = Strongly disagree

Another example that tries to get at the frequency of a problem be-havior would be the following scale:
I bring a weapon to school.

1. Never
2. Rarely
3. Sometimes
4. Often
5. Always

For younger children, you may want to use pictures of animals making gradations of emotional responses from very happy to sad, using happy faces and faces with frowns to choose. The Elementary Reading Attitude Survey uses such a scale (Rhodes 1992). Other attitude surveys have used cartoon characters such as Garfield in ranges of emotional reaction to help preliterate or children who have low literacy skills respond accord-ingly to a range of attitude questions. Even simply a smiling face for "yes" and a frowning face for "no" responses might be sufficient, and you can read the questions or statements aloud to the students.

Regardless of what method you use, guaranteeing confidentiality and having an established record of building trusting classroom relationships are very important to getting honest results.

Case Study Examples Using Informal Strategies

At WANTS (Weapons Are Not the Solution), I conducted observa-tions of students, teachers, and administrators in the classrooms, hallways, cafeteria, and other hot spots where violence was known to happen frequently. I also observed student behavior in their community centers and on the street corners. Violence, as I defined it, was a fairly regular part of the students' lives. Gangs surrounded the school. There were shootings outside. Some students refused to come to the school because they were afraid. Fights were common, but students did not usually find fighting particularly problematic, unless there was a threat of a fight extending beyond the school walls to involve gang members and weapons. In focus groups with students, they admitted that they were involved with gangs but, ironically, they felt gang membership and weapon carrying were essential to staying safe. Smoking marijuana and drinking at parties was a part of being social in a gang.

By contrast, the Deerfield students were concerned most about riding the bus. They admitted that fights were rare, but that teasing and put-downs were a problem. In my observations at Deerfield, I never saw any kind of physical violence and it was rare to see mean treatment by students. In my focus group discussions with students, they admitted that they felt safe for the most part, except sometimes on the bus with the older students. Some high school students drank and smoked marijuana regularly, and middle school students thought this behavior was problematic. At Deerfield, because it seemed that behaviors such as ostracism, put-downs, and mean treatment were the behaviors of primary concern for students, I created an informal survey based on the questions I developed as a result of the focus groups and interviews. (At WANTS, I used a formally developed and tested survey.)

Informal Survey for Deerfield and Result

In an effort to keep it simple for students, I selected a forced-choice, yes-no format. I was interested in most recent behavior such as hitting and fighting, but also their ability to calm themselves, if they felt good about themselves, and if they felt safe.

It was noteworthy that nearly a third of students did not feel safe on the bus. Also, nearly a third felt left out or ostracized by students on the playground and nearly half had been hit in school or on the bus. These numbers help give us a better idea of how widespread the perspectives and experiences are for students. As teachers or administrators, you can create simple, informal surveys such as this one that address your students' concerns.

Student Survey   Grade _____   Circle: Boy Girl
For teachers to read to students:
I would like to ask you a few questions about your experiences in school over the past
two months since you have had the *No Putdowns* program. Everything you say will be kept
secret, so you should not put your name on this survey. We want to figure out how
students are getting along in school so far this year, so we can make it better.
Please circle yes or no beside the question.

1. I know what a put-down is.	Yes	No
2. Students in this school sometimes use put-downs.	Yes	No
3. Students sometimes say mean things to me.	Yes	No
4. Students say mean things a lot in school.	Yes	No
5. Put-downs hurt my feelings.	Yes	No
6. Do you sometimes put others down or say mean things to others in school?	Yes	No
7. Do you feel safe in school?	Yes	No
8. Do you feel safe on the bus?	Yes	No
9. Do other students make you really angry in school?	Yes	No
10. Have you been in a fight in school during the past two months?	Yes	No
11. Have others picked on you on the bus in the past two months?	Yes	No
12. Do you feel left out when groups of students play on the playground?	Yes	No
13. Do you have a lot of friends at school?	Yes	No
14. Do you like school?	Yes	No
15. Are there groups of people you don't like in your school?	Yes	No
16. Are there people who are mean to other students in school or on the bus?	Yes	No
17. Do some people think you're mean in school or on the bus?	Yes	No
18. Do you get in trouble in class?	Yes	No
19. Do you think you're a good student?	Yes	No
20. Do you like most of your classes?	Yes	No
21. Do you get in trouble a lot at home?	Yes	No
22. Have you hit anyone at school or on the bus in the past two months?	Yes	No
23. Have you been hit in school or on the bus in the past two months?	Yes	No
24. Can you calm down when someone makes you very upset?	Yes	No
25. Can you list many things you are good at doing?	Yes	No

The students' perspectives and issues are quite different at WANTS and Deerfield as we examine them using informal strategies such as interviews, focus groups, and informal surveys. Interviews and focus groups yield a depth of information in the students' own words, which allows us to better understand what kinds of violence they deal with on a regular basis, and what strategies they use to try to keep themselves safe. Informal surveys give us a picture of the students' perspectives and issues. We need to have a better understanding of students' perspectives before we choose programs to address their needs. Informal strategies

---

Deerfield Middle School Pretest Results for the Sixth Grade

Student Survey   Grade ___6___   Circle: Boy (55) Girl (72)
For teachers to read to students: N = 128
I would like to ask you a few questions about your experiences in school over the past two months. Everything you say will be kept secret, so you should not put your name on this survey. We want to figure out how students are getting along in school so far this year, so we can make it better.
Please circle yes or no beside the question.

	Yes	No
1. I know what a put-down is.	99.2%	.8%
2. Students in this school sometimes use put-downs.	92.2	7.8
3. Students sometimes say mean things to me.	72.7	27.3
4. Students say mean things a lot in school.	52.3	47.7
5. Put-downs hurt my feelings.	82.8	17.2
6. Do you sometimes put others down or say mean things to others in school?	39.4	60.6
7. Do you feel safe in school?	89.1	10.9
8. Do you feel safe on the bus?	70.4	29.6
9. Do other students make you really angry in school?	48.4	51.6
10. Have you been in a fight in school during the past two months?	23.4	76.6
11. Have others picked on you on the bus in the past two months?	23.4	76.6
12. Do you feel left out when groups of students play on the playground?	31.3	68.8
13. Do you have a lot of friends at school?	90.6	9.4
14. Do you like school?	83.3	16.7
15. Are there groups of people you don't like in your school?	81.1	18.9
16. Are there people who are mean to other students in school or on the bus?	88.1	11.9
17. Do some people think you're mean in school or on the bus?	18.5	81.5
18. Do you get in trouble in class?	12.6	87.4
19. Do you think you're a good student?	89.0	11.0
20. Do you like most of your classes?	88.2	11.8
21. Do you get in trouble a lot at home?	25.2	74.8
22. Have you hit anyone at school or on the bus in the past two months?	22.2	77.8
23. Have you been hit in school or on the bus in the past two months?	45.7	54.3
24. Can you calm down when someone makes you very upset?	85.6	14.4
25. Can you list many things you are good at doing?	94.5	5.5

allow us access to this information in a way that is relatively inexpensive although time intensive, making collaboration helpful.

How to Formalize Informal Strategies

With purposeful qualitative analysis strategies, one can formalize the above data-collection strategies. More formal analysis includes the keeping of notes during observations, interviews, and focus groups and analyzing the text for themes or categories that emerge. What common categories or themes do you see emerging in your notes? Do students consistently describe a fear of riding the bus, ostracism based on their lack of athletic ability, or struggles resisting illegal behavior associated with gang membership? Are there interesting topics that keep emerging into which you would like to delve deeper and ask more probing questions or do more specific observations? These qualitative data-analysis strategies will formalize your data-gathering strategies and will be useful for triangulation (using a variety of sources to confirm or deny your findings).

FORMAL STRATEGIES

There are many formally developed and tested surveys to measure problem behavior in the school. These often cost money and take a fair amount of time to administer to the whole school, but may sometimes be less labor intensive because you do not need to craft them yourself. It is also often less time intensive to administer a schoolwide, formal survey (although analyzing the data can be labor intensive) than to interview and conduct focus groups. However, the information is different. As described earlier, the observation, interview, focus group, and student journal yield a depth of information in a student's own words whereas the survey gives us a breadth of information about the extent of violence-related problems.

It is usually necessary that you get parental consent before giving formal surveys to children under age eighteen. Depending on your school district's policy, you may be required to obtain what is called "passive consent" (sending parents a letter explaining the survey, how the results will be used, and how their child will be protected). Some districts require "active consent," which is written permission from parents in response to a letter describing the project, the potential for harm, and the rationale for conducting the survey. Regardless, letting parents know that you will be having students complete a survey is important.

Some examples of formal strategies to measure problem behavior include:

- Adaptive Behavior Inventory (ABI)
- Walker Problem Behavior Identification Checklist

- Walker-McConnell Scale of Social Competence and School Adjustment
- Child Behavior Checklist (Achenbach)

Your school psychologist should have a variety of formal measures of problem behavior.

Other formally tested surveys dealing with school violence:

- Centers for Disease Control's Youth Risk Behavior Surveillance Survey—also known as the YRBSS (ordering information available at www.cdc.gov)
- Hamilton Fish's National School Crime and Safety Survey (ordering information available at www.hamfish.org)
- The Oregon School Safety Survey Assessment of Risk Factors (Sprague, Colvin, and Irvin 1995)

Formal as well as informal strategies can be used to help with the following important activities.

Examining risk factors such as those identified by:

- American Medical Association
- American Psychological Association
- Office of Juvenile Justice and Delinquency Prevention

Examining warning signs for psychological classifications:

- Conduct Disorder
- Oppositional Defiance Disorder
- Antisocial Personality Disorder
- Emotional Disturbance
- Posttraumatic Stress Disorder
- Grief
- Depression
- Suicide
- Self-mutilation

Examining other underreported problem behaviors:

- Bullying/teasing/ostracizing
- Relational aggression

- Intimate partner violence
- Sexual harassment
- Child abuse

FORMAL SURVEYS TO MEASURE PROBLEM BEHAVIOR

Special educators and school psychologists have been trained to examine "adaptive behavior" of children with aggression problems, and youth at risk of violence. Special educators are an excellent resource to help examine individual students you suspect may have adaptive behavior problems, conduct disorders, or other more severe behavioral or emotional problems. Special educators are often trained to conduct functional behavior assessments that examine the function a disruptive or violent behavior serves. In addition, there are other popular inventories used by special educators to determine at-risk, potentially violent behavior: the Adaptive Behavior Inventory (Brown and Leigh 1986), the Walker Problem Behavior Identification Checklist (Walker 1983), and the more recent Walker-McConnell Scale of Social Competence and School Adjustment (Walker and McConnell 1995). The special education expert in your school should also know many others. There are clinical surveys examining student behavior that have used comparison populations and created norms and tested for reliability and validity. For more information, see *Assessment of Exceptional Students: Educational and Psychological Procedures* (Taylor 2000).

The Centers for Disease Control (www.cdc.gov) has a comprehensive Youth Risk Behavior Surveillance Survey. The CDC administers this inventory regularly to schools around the country to determine the extent of such problem behaviors as school crime (including violence), drug abuse, and other risky behaviors. Some researchers have challenged the reliability and validity of the YRBSS, so it should be used cautiously and results analyzed with care (Furlong and Morrison 2002).

At WANTS, because it was to be included in a national study of which I was a part, we used the National School Crime and Safety Survey developed by the Hamilton Fish National Institute on School and Community Violence (for more information and a copy of the staff and student surveys, see http://hamfish.org/pub/natsur.html). For a copy of some of the questions and results from the student pretest survey, see table 2.3.

Table 2.3.   Selected Questions and Percentages of Response from the *National School Crime and Safety Survey* Student Pretest Administered at WANTS 1998

What grade are you in?

	7th	8th	9th	10th	11th	12th
Frequency	11	8	11	7	4	2
Percentage	25.6	18.6	25.6	16.3	9.3	4.7

What sex are you?

	Male	Female
Frequency	15	28
Percentage	34.9	65.1

Racial breakdown
(Note: Respondents could mark more than one answer so percentages were not calculated)

	African American	White	Hispanic	Native American	Asian
Frequency	30	7	5	9	1

I can keep from getting really angry.

	Strongly agree	Agree	Neither	Disagree	Strongly disagree
Frequency	5	10	9	5	10
Percent	12.8	25.6	23.1	12.8	25.6

Do your parents think you should get into trouble if you behave violently at school?

	Yes	No	Don't Know
Frequency	19	7	16
Percent	45.2	16.7	38.1

I would fight if someone tried to start a fight with me.

	Strongly agree	Agree	Neither	Disagree	Strongly disagree
Frequency	9	16	7	8	1
Percent	22	39	17.1	19.5	2.4

I would fight if someone spread rumors about me.

	Strongly agree	Agree	Neither	Disagree	Strongly disagree
Frequency	12	7	14	4	2
Percent	30.8	17.9	35.9	10.3	5.1

I would fight if someone disrespected or insulted me.

	Strongly agree	Agree	Neither	Disagree	Strongly disagree
Frequency	15	11	7	5	2
Percent	37.5	27.5	17.5	12.5	5

I would fight if someone insulted a member of my family.

	Strongly agree	Agree	Neither	Disagree	Strongly disagree
Frequency	13	11	5	5	4
Percent	34.2	28.9	13.2	13.2	10.5

I would fight if someone damaged my property.

	Strongly agree	Agree	Neither	Disagree	Strongly disagree
Frequency	13	15	6	2	2
Percent	34.2	39.5	15.8	5.3	5.3

I would fight if someone hurt someone I care about.

	Strongly agree	Agree	Neither	Disagree	Strongly disagree
Frequency	13	15	79	1	2
Percent	32.5	37.5	22.5	2.5	5.0

I can ignore someone who insults or disrespects me.

	Yes	No	Don't Know
Frequency	14	19	7
Percent	35	47.5	17.5

How effective are the following ways to avoid violence in school: Letting others know that you will fight if you have to

	Very effective	Somewhat effective	Not very effective
Frequency	24	9	10
Percent	55.8	20.5	23.3

How effective are the following ways to avoid violence in school: Joining a gang

	Very effective	Somewhat effective	Not very effective
Frequency	10	8	23
Percent	24.4	19.5	56.1

continued

Table 2.3. Selected Questions and Percentages of Response from the *National School Crime and Safety Survey* Student Pretest Administered at WANTS 1998 (*continued*)

How effective are the following ways to avoid violence in school: Involving adults

	Very effective	Somewhat effective	Not very effective
Frequency	9	22	10
Percent	22.0	53.7	24.4

Victimization at school: In the past week the number of times somebody hit, punched, or slapped you

	Never	1–2 times	3–5 times	10 or more times
Frequency	30	6	3	3
Percent	71.4	14.3	7.1	7.1

Victimization at school: In the past week the number of times somebody pushed or shoved you

	Never	1–2 times	3–5 times	10 or more times
Frequency	31	7	1	3
Percent	73.8	16.7	2.4	7.1

Perpetration at school: In the past week the number of times you hit, punched, or slapped someone else

	Never	1–2 times	3–5 times	10 or more times
Frequency	31	8	3	0
Percent	73.8	19.0	7.1	0

Perpetration at school: In the past week the number of times you pushed or shoved someone else

	Never	1–2 times	3–5 times	10 or more times
Frequency	33	6	1	1
Percent	80.5	14.6	2.4	2.4

Witnessed at school: In the past week the number of times you watched a severe beating

	Never	1–2 times	3–5 times	6–9 times	10 or more times
Frequency	18	13	3	5	2
Percent	43.9	31.7	7.3	12.2	4.9

Witnessed at school: In the past week the number of times you witnessed a sexual assault

	Never	1–2 times	3–5 times	6–9 times	10 or more times
Frequency	31	7	2	0	2
Percent	73.8	16.7	4.8	0	4.8

Witnessed at school: Knife

	Never	1–2 times	3–5 times	6–9 times	10 or more times
Frequency	16	11	6	3	5
Percent	39	26.8	14.6	7.3	12.2

Witnessed at school: Gun

	Never	1–2 times	3–5 times	6–9 times	10 or more times
Frequency	23	15	0	2	2
Percent	54.8	35.7	0	4.8	4.8

Are you in a gang?

	Yes	No
Frequency	11	27
Percentage	28.9	71.1

Does your gang have violent initiations?

	Yes	No
Frequency	5	6
Percentage	45.5	54.5

Does your gang use drugs?

	Yes	No
Frequency	3	7
Percentage	27.3	63.6

The National School Crime and Safety Survey was administered in September 1998 to students at the alternative school. Items on the survey asked students to respond to statements about their experiences with violence in school as perpetrators, witnesses, and victims (fighting, shoving, punching); the strategies they used to avoid violence in school; and their gang involvement. Pretest and posttest surveys were used in conjunction with other informal data collected. In the alternative school, forty-three students in grades 7 through 12 completed the pretest questionnaire. Seventy percent of the students were in grades 7 through 9; 35 percent of the students were males and 65 percent females.

Among some of the important findings were that only 38 percent of students reported that they could keep from getting really angry. Sixty-five percent of students agreed or strongly agreed with the statement that they would get into a fight if someone disrespected them. More than half reported that they had witnessed at least one severe beating in school in the past month. Nearly one-third of the students admitted to being involved with a gang. Nearly half of gang-involved students admitted that their gangs had violent initiations and nearly a third reported that their gang used drugs. Using a more formal survey gave a good picture of the extent of gang involvement, drug abuse, and violent activity. For more details about the results from this survey, see table 2.3 or http://education.cortland.edu/~williams for more articles and information by the author from this project.

This information became useful when evaluating the impact of programs on the students as well as establishing the needs of the students. Clearly, there were problems with gangs. There were also problems with students fighting over issues of "respect." Programs were put in place to address these specific issues and help students deal constructively with conflict and anger. These data helped determine the impact of the program. Were they less likely to get in a fight if someone disrespected them? Were they less likely to become involved with a gang as a result of the program? Having baseline data of this nature made this evaluation much easier and more useful.

RISK FACTORS AND WARNING SIGNS

Both formal and informal strategies help identify students at risk of violent behavior. Early identification is critical to prevention. However, a word of caution: just because a student is identified as "at risk," he or she should not be ostracized or victimized. Students in need of support services should receive them. Creating a plan that involves the student (once identified), his or her family, and a caseworker, social worker, counselor, or special educator must also be a part of any plan. In addition, research literature has demonstrated that risk factors may be poor predictors of future violence (see Furlong, Bates, and Smith 2001). The following section summarizes some of the research findings on risk factors as well as warning signs of psychological problems that are sometimes associated with violent behaviors in schools and signs of other underreported forms of violence.

Office of Juvenile Justice and Delinquency Prevention

The Office of Juvenile Justice and Delinquency Prevention commissioned a report by Hawkins et al. (2000) that broke down risk factors by individual factors, family factors, school factors, peer-related factors, and community and neighborhood factors. They examined the research literature on youth violence in an attempt to identify some factors that put children at risk of violent and destructive criminal behavior. In this comprehensive report, they identified the following risk factors.

Individual factors:

- Pregnancy and delivery complications when the student was born
- Low resting heart rate
- Internalizing disorders (nervousness, withdrawal, worrying, and anxiety)
- Hyperactivity, concentration problems, restlessness, and risk taking
- Aggressiveness
- Early initiation of violent behavior
- Involvement in other forms of antisocial behavior
- Beliefs and attitudes favorable to deviant or antisocial behavior

Family factors:

- Parent criminality
- Child maltreatment
- Poor family management practices
- Low levels of parental involvement
- Poor family bonding and family conflict
- Parental attitudes favorable to substance abuse and violence
- Parent-child separation

School factors:

- Academic failure
- Low bonding to school
- Truancy and dropping out of school
- Frequent school transitions

Peer-related factors:

- Delinquent siblings
- Delinquent peers
- Gang membership

Community and neighborhood factors:

- Poverty
- Community disorganization
- Availability of drugs and firearms
- Neighborhood adults involved in crime
- Exposure to violence and racial prejudice

These risk factors have been associated with violence in schools, although all are not created equal. This list should not be used as a checklist where children with more of these risk factors are at higher risk for violence than those with none. For more information about each of these factors, the research conducted, and their relationship to youth violence, please consult the Hawkins et al. (2000) report.

The American Psychological Association (APA) Risk Factors

The American Psychological Association (reprinted from www. apa.org) offered the following risk factors to help educators identify youth at risk of violence:

- A history of violent or aggressive behavior
- Serious drug or alcohol use

- Gang membership or strong desire to be in a gang
- Access to or fascination with weapons, especially guns
- Threatening others
- Regular trouble controlling feelings like anger, or withdrawal from friends and usual activities
- Feeling rejected or alone
- Having been a victim of bullying
- Poor school performance
- History of discipline problems or frequent run-ins with authority
- Feeling constantly disrespected
- Failing to acknowledge the feelings or rights of others
  (List reprinted from http://helping.apa.org/warningsigns/ recognizing.html)

American Academy of Child and Adolescent Psychiatry's Warning Signs

According to the American Academy of Child and Adolescent Psychiatry, there are different psychological classifications used in schools to classify children with aggressive behaviors or a group of other problem behaviors. Table 2.4 describes three classifications that may be associated with violent behavior in schools: oppositional defiant disorder (ODD), conduct disorder (CD), and antisocial personality disorder.

In addition to these three classifications, there is another classification for aggressive youth used in schools: emotional disturbance (ED). Special educators typically use this term to classify students who have chronic emotional conditions that interfere with their ability to participate in the traditional educational system. These students typically have behavioral and social interactions that are developmentally behind and make concentrating and functioning in the more typical classroom challenging.

Conduct disorder, oppositional defiance, antisocial personality, and emotional disturbance include problem behaviors that are more obviously associated with youth at risk of violence in schools. In addition to these more overt behaviors, we need to examine those behaviors that may be less obvious, but can be just as troubling and problematic.

Table 2.4.   American Academy of Child and Adolescent Psychiatry: Labels of Psychological Classifications for Childhood Aggressive Disorders

Oppositional Defiant Disorder	Conduct Disorder	Antisocial Personality Disorder
Loses temper	Aggression to people, animals	Evidence of conduct disorder prior to age 15
Argues with adults	Bullies, threatens, intimidates, uses dangerous weapons, physically cruel to people and animals, forced into sex	Failure to conform to social norms
Refuses adult requests	Destruction of property	Deceitfulness
Does things to annoy	Fire setting	Impulsivity
Blames others for own mistakes	Stealing with confrontation	Irritability
Touchy, easily annoyed, angry, resentful	Deliberate destruction of property	Physical aggression
Spiteful, vindictive, vengeful	Theft and serious violation of rules	Reckless disregard for safety of others
Initiates confrontations— more likely with adults and others the child knows well	Steals, lies, runs away, truant Serious and consistent violation of rules	Consistent irresponsibility Lack of remorse
Onset before age 8 to early adolescence	Six month duration Onset usually prepuberty	Classification at 18 years Usually has label of ODD and CD
Childhood/adolescence 2–16% of the population	Childhood/adolescence 2–16% male 2–9% female	Adulthood 3% males 1% females

Adapted from information provided on their website. More information is available from their website by searching for the following psychiatric disorders http://www.aacap.org

Risk Factors for More Concealed Psychological Classifications

Other psychological classifications are associated with children at risk of violence but their behaviors may be somewhat more concealed (quiet, sad, or withdrawn) than those described above—including the often-omitted forms of violence to the self as well as grief and depression. The following will be discussed briefly here: posttraumatic stress disorder, grief, depression, self-mutilation, and suicide.

Posttraumatic stress disorder.   One psychological classification that might be present among at-risk youth is posttraumatic stress disorder (PTSD). Children with PTSD may show the following symptoms (reprinted from American Academy of Child and Adolescent Psychiatry at www.aacap.org/publications/factsFam/ptsd70.htm):

- Worry about dying at an early age
- Losing interest in activities
- Having physical symptoms such as headaches and stomachaches
- Showing more sudden and extreme emotional reactions
- Having problems falling or staying asleep
- Showing irritability or angry outbursts
- Having problems concentrating
- Acting younger than their age (e.g., clingy or whiny behavior, thumb sucking)
- Showing increased alertness to the environment
- Repeating behavior that reminds them of the trauma

Children who are victims of violence are at high risk of becoming perpetrators of violence. These same children may likely experience PTSD as a result of the violence they have experienced.

Grief and loss.   In addition, many children in high-risk neighborhoods experience a great deal of loss in their lives (death of loved ones, friends, family, etc.) and have no outlet for their grief. Children at WANTS, for example, missed a lot of school to attend funerals and wakes for loved ones. They witnessed death on the streets and in their homes, some on a fairly regular basis, with no opportunities for psychological help to deal with their grief. The American Academy of Child and Adolescent Psychiatry listed the following signs of a child having difficulty with loss (reprinted from www.aacap.org/publications/factsFam/grief.htm):

- An extended period of depression in which the child loses interest in daily activities and events
- Inability to sleep, loss of appetite, prolonged fear of being alone
- Acting much younger for an extended period
- Excessively imitating the dead person
- Repeated statements of wanting to join the dead person
- Withdrawal from friends
- Sharp drop in school performance or refusal to attend school

Some students who experience a great deal of loss may hide these feelings. If you know that a student has experienced a loss or frequent loss, it is important to consider that the child might need help dealing with his or her grief.

Depression.   The American Academy of Child and Adolescent Psychiatrists (www.aacap.org) identified the following warning signs for depression:

- Frequent sadness, tearfulness, crying
- Hopelessness
- Decreased interest in activities or an inability to enjoy previously favorite activities
- Persistent boredom, low energy
- Social isolation, poor communication
- Low self-esteem and guilt
- Extreme sensitivity to rejection or failure
- Increased irritability, anger, or hostility
- Difficulty with relationships
- Frequent complaints of physical illnesses such as headaches and stomachaches
- Frequent absences from school or poor performance in school
- Poor concentration
- A major change in eating or sleeping patterns
- Talk of or efforts to run away from home
- Thoughts or expressions of suicide or self-destructive behavior

Children with warning signs of depression are also at risk of violence against themselves or others. Children feeling chronic despair or depression may feel as though they have nothing to lose by acting out any aggressive fantasies. Psychological help should be made available to students showing consistent signs of depression.

Risk Factors for Harming Oneself

Depending on your own personal definition of violence (whether or not it includes harm to the self), you may not think about such behaviors as suicide and self-mutilation when thinking about violence. However, these forms of violence turned inward are very significant, harmful, and lethal types of violence that need to be considered in our discussions of violence and our examination of risk factors that students display.

Suicide. Suicide is a tragedy that affects many young people, their family, and other loved ones. Threats of suicide should be taken very seriously to determine the severity of the threat. It is important to determine if the child making the threat has the means to commit suicide. It is important to seek professional psychological help immediately when a child makes threats of suicide. The American Academy of Child and Adolescent Psychiatry offers the following signs or risk factors for youth at risk of committing suicide (reprinted from www.aacap.org/publications/factsFam/suicide.htm).

- Change in eating and sleeping habits
- Withdrawal from friends, family, and regular activities
- Violent actions, rebellious behavior, or running away
- Drug and alcohol use
- Unusual neglect of personal appearance
- Marked personality change
- Persistent boredom, difficulty concentrating, or a decline in the quality of schoolwork
- Frequent complaints about physical symptoms, often related to emotions, such as stomachaches, headaches, fatigue, etc.
- Loss of interest in pleasurable activities
- Not tolerating praise or rewards

A teenager who is planning to commit suicide may also:

- Complain of being a bad person or feeling "rotten inside"
- Give verbal hints with statements such as, "I won't be a problem for you much longer," "Nothing matters," "It's no use," and "I won't see you again."
- Put his or her affairs in order; for example, give away favorite possessions, clean his or her room, throw away important belongings, etc.
- Become suddenly cheerful after a period of depression
- Have signs of psychosis (hallucinations or bizarre thoughts)

If a child or adolescent says, "I want to kill myself" or "I'm going to commit suicide," always take the statement seriously and seek evaluation from a child and adolescent psychiatrist or other physician. People often feel uncomfortable talking about death. However, asking the child or adolescent whether he or she is depressed or thinking about suicide can be helpful. Rather than "putting thoughts in the child's head," such a question will provide assurance that somebody cares and will give the young person the chance to talk about problems.

Self-mutilation.   Self-mutilation (sometimes referred to as self-injury) includes behaviors that are physically harmful or damaging to oneself (biting, carving, burning, hitting, bruising, etc.). These behaviors may be symptomatic of other psychological illnesses, but may be a way for children to deal with stress, anger, frustration, or low self-esteem. For more information on self-mutilation or self-injury, see the American Academy of Child and Adolescent Psychiatry's website at www.aacap. org/publications/factsFam/73.htm.

Teachers and administrators need to be on the lookout for these less overt warning signs of forms of violence (PTSD, grief, depression, etc.) as well as remaining vigilant for more overt warning signs of the other psychological classifications described (conduct disorder, oppositional defiance, etc.). Immediate referral to appropriate mental health staff in schools or outside agencies is critical. It is important to remember that school psychologists and special educators are experts in identifying all of the behaviors listed above and in helping students receive appropriate services. Work with a team of psychological specialists to make sure that students receive appropriate services, and follow up with the service providers as well as the student and his or her family to make sure that the assistance is making a positive difference.

A Word of Caution about Risk Factors

Risk factors have been shown to be ineffective and inappropriate to predict future violent behavior of children—resulting in many children being inappropriately labeled (Furlong, Bates, and Smith 2001). Be careful that you never use these risk factors to label, exclude, stereotype, or punish a child but rather consider these factors as a part of a whole context including a child, family, school, and larger community. Risk factors might be used to identify appropriate services for students. One risk factor, or even a couple, does not mean a student will be violent. These risk factors should be taken within the whole-school context and as a part of the student within that context. These are not absolute predictors of violent behavior, so please be careful with their use.

OTHER UNDERREPORTED PROBLEM BEHAVIORS

For children, some violent acts have become accepted as part of the status quo. Bullying, ostracizing, teasing, relational aggression among girls, sexual harassment, and dating/relationship violence are among the problem behaviors that young people often accept as a part of the norm and fail to report. As part of your examination of the problems your students face, it becomes necessary to keep a special lookout for these types of problems.

Bullying, Teasing, and Ostracizing

According to researchers, bullying has come to be defined in two ways—direct and indirect. Direct bullying refers to the more overt, more obvious forms of problem behavior such as put-downs, teasing, taunting, threatening, hitting, and stealing that can be perpetrated by one or more children against another selected victim. Indirect bullying is less likely to be seen or reported because it is often accepted by children as "just the way it is." These less obvious forms of indirect bullying are purposeful exclusion and ostracizing behavior (described in the following section on "relational aggression"). According to Banks (1997),

> While boys typically engage in direct bullying methods, girls who bully are more apt to utilize these more subtle indirect strategies, such as spreading rumors and enforcing social isolation (Ahmad and Smith 1994; Smith and Sharp 1994). Whether the bullying is direct or indirect, the key component of bullying is that the physical or psychological intimidation occurs repeatedly over time to create an ongoing pattern of harassment and abuse (Batsche and Knoff 1994; Olweus 1993).

The data from Deerfield show us that teasing and put-downs as well as bullying behavior are widespread and problematic in schools. The good news is that if we work to reduce these behaviors, we can reduce forms of physical violence as well. Increasing awareness is a start to reducing these problem behaviors.

Relational Aggression and Its Special Role with Girls

Based on the research on bullying that demonstrates that girls are more likely to engage in forms of indirect bullying, the patterns of these more subtle forms of aggression have been examined. Girls have been found to engage in distinctly different forms of aggression that have now been termed relational aggression. Annette Klinefelter is executive director of the Girls' Initiative Network in Portland, Oregon, and conducts workshops and training programs designed specifically to address the issues of relational aggression. She stated that girls have been found to have "distinctive friendship patterns that revolve around shifting, didactic alliances which are jealously guarded and reflect the notions of exclusivity, intensity, intimacy, and disclosure" (2002, 9). These friendship patterns result in girls purposely ganging up on other girls to ostracize them. They treat other girls, often ones who were once close friends, cruelly. She states that girls who are involved in relational aggression are at risk for a host of personal problems such as truancy and other delinquent behaviors, as well as depression and other emotional problems.

The specific problems that girls face need to be addressed in schools because this kind of relational aggression is often overlooked as "just the way it is" or as just typical female "cattiness" that is socially acceptable. Getting girls to examine the nature of their cruelty in their relationships is part of beginning to address the problem. For more information and strategies, see www.girlsinitiativenetwork.org.

Sexual Harassment

In many school settings, students have come to not only tolerate sexual harassment but also accept it as a part of going to school. Girls have learned to accept having their body parts pinched and fondled, and hearing comments about their sexuality and body parts. Some of the most regular forms of teasing I've heard have been comments, particularly among boys, about one's sexuality—using such terms as "faggot" or "queer."

In observations and focus groups in my own work, students have come to define sexual harassment to only include physical behaviors that are actually forms of sexual assault (e.g., unwanted sexual touching or the use of force in a sexual way). We need to include verbal forms of sexual harassment in our own definitions and examine the experiences that our students have with lesser-reported forms of sexual harassment (e.g., sexual teasing and unwanted sexual comments).

Schools must be concerned with sexual harassment. The following legal decisions (available online at www.ed.gov/offices/OCR/shguide/index.html) have had a profound impact on how courts view the role of the school in both student-to-student harassment as well as teacher-to-student harassment:

> The Supreme Court (Court) has issued several important decisions in sexual harassment cases, including two decisions specifically addressing sexual harassment of students under Title IX: *Gebser v. Lago Vista Independent School District* (Gebser), 524 U.S. 274 (1998), and *Davis v. Monroe County Board of Education* (Davis), 526 U.S. 629 (1999). The Court held in Gebser that a school can be liable for monetary damages if a teacher sexually harasses a student, an official who has authority to address the harassment has actual knowledge of the harassment, and that official is deliberately indifferent in responding to the harassment. In Davis, the Court announced that a school also may be liable for monetary damages if one student sexually harasses another student in the school's program and the conditions of Gebser are met (Office of Civil Rights 2002).

Schools have a legal as well as a moral obligation to protect children from sexual harassment. We need to be on the lookout for it because sexual harassment has become so much a part of daily life in schools that students often do not recognize it. Therefore, we must employ both informal and formal means to determine the nature and extent of sexual harassment in school.

Relationship/Dating Violence

Young women between the ages of sixteen and twenty-four are at highest risk of experiencing violence at the hands of their boyfriends or partners. This kind of violence has received many titles—relationship,

dating, or intimate partner violence. According to the U.S. Bureau of
Crime Statistics, "Younger women generally had higher rates of intimate
partner violence than older women. The 1999 per capita rate of intimate
partner violence against women was 6 victimizations per 1,000; per
1,000 females age 16–24, it was 16 victimizations, and per 1,000 females
age 25–34, 9 victimizations" (available online at www.ojp.usdoj.gov; the
full text of the document is available at www.ojp.usdoj.gov/bjs/pub/pdf/
ipva99.pdf).

Tjaden and Thoennes (1998) wrote a comprehensive report for the
U.S. Department of Justice highlighted in their journal on intimate partner violence. The report highlights the risk for young women and includes some advice about wording survey questions to get at this often
underreported kind of violence.

Understandably, colleges have been interested in better understanding and identifying young women at risk of relationship/intimate partner/
dating violence because the traditional college-age group is at highest
risk. However, those in secondary education should be looking out for
warning signs as well. Because it is often not discussed in middle and
high schools, this problem tends to be silenced and girls are not aware of
it, or come to accept it as normal.

The University of Buffalo's Counseling Center (2002) has a website
(http://ub-counseling.buffalo.edu/warnings.html) with helpful links and
information as well as signs of problematic relationships or relationships
at risk for violence. They offer the following warning signs for young
women in intimate relationships:

- Emotionally abuses you (insults, belittling comments, ignoring you,
  acting sulky or angry when you initiate an action or idea).
- Tells you whom you may be friends with, how you should dress, or
  tries to control other elements of your life or relationships.
- Talks negatively about women in general.
- Gets jealous when there is no reason.
- Drinks heavily, uses drugs, or tries to get you drunk.
- Berates you for not wanting to get drunk, get high, have sex, or go
  with him to an isolated or personal place.
- Refuses to let you share any of the expenses of a date and gets an-
  gry when you offer to pay.

- Is physically violent to you or others, even if it's "just" grabbing and pushing to get his way.
- Acts in an intimidating way toward you by invading your "personal space" (sits too close, speaks as if he knows you much better than he does, touches you when you tell him not to).
- Is unable to handle sexual and emotional frustrations without becoming angry.
- Does not view you as an equal—because he's older or sees himself as smarter or socially superior.
- Thinks poorly of himself and guards his masculinity by acting tough.
- Goes through extreme highs and lows, is kind one minute and cruel the next.
- Is angry and threatening to the extent that you have changed your life so as not to anger him.

Child Abuse and the Victim-Perpetration Cycle

Child abuse is violence. Although this book does not focus on issues of child abuse, it deserves special mention. Teachers and administrators are always on the lookout for signs of child abuse because it is mandated that they report any suspicion of child abuse and neglect. In addition, victims of violence are at high risk of becoming perpetrators; some children who experience violence in the home may come to school and become perpetrators of violence against others.

New York State (from http://child-abuse.com) has defined child abuse as:

An abused child is one who is under 18 years of age whose parent—or other person legally responsible for his/her care—inflicts or allows to be inflicted upon the child physical injury by other than accidental means, or creates or allows to be created a substantial risk of physical injury by other than accidental means, which would be likely to cause death or serious or protracted disfigurement, or protracted impairment of physical or emotional health or protracted loss or impairment of the function of any bodily organ.

Children who are victims at home are at high risk of becoming perpetrators in other settings such as school. I saw this a lot at WANTS.

The overwhelming majority of students at WANTS had experienced some form of abuse in the home. One of the first questions you should ask yourself when you encounter a violent child is, "Where might this child fall victim to violence?" Sometimes, these same violent children are treated cruelly in school or on their way to or from school. However, in many cases you can trace the victimization to the child's home. According to statistics compiled by Prevent Child Abuse New York (2002):

> Nationwide, in the last decade of the millennium, the number of children reported as abused or neglected in the United States grew by 33 percent to reach a level of 3,244,000, according to a report released by Prevent Child Abuse America. That is a rate of 46 of every 1,000 children in the population. The number of confirmed cases of child abuse and neglect was estimated at 1,070,000 in 1999, a rate of 15 of every 1,000 children in the population. This study is based on information provided by child protective service agencies in 46 states, representing 96.2 percent of total U.S. child population.

Clearly, child abuse is a pervasive problem in our society. This kind of violence in the home has an impact on violence in our schools. Children who might be victims of child abuse may behave violently in school as bullies or consistent perpetrators. Sometimes, victims at home are victims at school. Sometimes victims are silent. We need to look critically at who the perpetrators and the victims are—it's not always clear.

Teachers and administrators, as mandated reporters, must know what is expected of them and must be able to recognize the signs of child abuse. Prevent Child Abuse New York has warning signs and definitions that are reprinted in table 2.5. These are also available on their website available at http://child-abuse.com.

Many states require teachers and administrators to take a child abuse reporting workshop before becoming certified to teach. Workshops such as these are very helpful and informative but usually only scratch the surface. For more information on signs of child abuse, the role of the mandated reporter, and definitions, see http://child-abuse.com.

Table 2.5.   Definitions and Ways of Recognizing Child Abuse

Types of Abuse	What does that mean?	How do I recognize It?
Physical Abuse	A non-accidental injury to a child by a parent or caretaker.	You may see frequent and unexplained bruises, burns, cuts, injuries; the child may be overly afraid of the parent's reaction to misbehavior.
Physical Neglect	A parent or caretaker's failure to give the child food, clothing, hygiene, medical care and supervision.	You may see a very young child routinely left alone at home. You may know that a severe illness or injury is not being medically treated. A neighbor child may frequently turn up at your door—inadequately dressed for the weather—saying their parent told them to stay away. Physical neglect can be hard to judge; sometimes what you see is poor judgment, but not neglect. Sometimes what you see is the result of poverty, not parental neglect.
Sexual Abuse	Ranges from offenses such as promoting prostitution, to fondling, intercourse, or using the child for pornographic materials.	You may observe sexual behavior way beyond what is expected for the child's age; a young child might have sudden, unusual difficulty with toilet habits; there may be pain or itching, bruises or bleeding in the genital area. The child might tell you.
Emotional Abuse	Includes severe rejection, humiliation, and actions intended to produce fear or extreme guilt in a child.	You may see a parent who verbally terrorizes the child, who continually and severely criticizes the child, or who fails to express any affection or nurturing

Reprinted from http://child-abuse.com

PROTECTIVE FACTORS

Any discussion of risk factors and warning signs must include a reflection on protective factors. Protective factors may buffer risk factors from having a negative impact on a child. Teachers and administrators can use information on risk factors to identify student needs and assess the ability of programs or program components to address these needs. However, it is also important to identify protective factors that promote successful development.

Three key factors that have been identified as fostering the development of resiliency (*School Staff Guide* 1997):

1. Caring and support (e.g., creating caring, cooperative classrooms, mentoring opportunities)
2. High expectations (e.g., having high expectations of student performance in your classrooms)
3. Opportunities for meaningful participation and a sense of bonding to the school (e.g., helping students feel a part of the classroom community, participating in cocurricular and classroom activities)

Hawkins, Catalano, and Miller (1992) identified the following protective factors that reduce a student's risk of substance abuse that may also place students at risk of school violence:

1. Individual characteristics: Some students have more resilient temperaments—accepting disappointment well and not letting themselves get hurt easily. These children are the ones who seem to adapt to challenging situations. Students who have positive peers and positive role models are also at reduced risk.
2. Bonding: Students with strong positive bonds to and relationships with their families, friends, school, and community are at lower risk. These students tend to set and work to achieve goals valued by those with whom they have positive relationships. School has a role in helping them achieve their goals. Students with constant school failure often create goals that they feel do not include academic success (e.g., dancer, rap musician, homemaker, professional athlete). These students often do not feel bonded to school because of academic failure that began early in their school careers. Getting children bonded and able to see the important role of school in their futures is important to building resiliency.
3. Healthy beliefs and clear standards: Students who have schools, families, or peers who teach them healthy beliefs and enforce clear standard for behavior, such as being drug free, eating healthfully, exercising and taking care of one's body, being community oriented, respectful of others, focused on learning, and being strong academically, will be at reduced risk for violence.

WHAT YOU CAN DO

The previously listed behaviors demonstrate behaviors that have been associated with students being put at risk of violent behavior as well as factors that have been found to protect students against these risk factors. As teachers or administrators, you should be prepared to:

- Thoughtfully and carefully recognize these at-risk behaviors as a tool for getting help or services for youth who could best benefit from services.
- Work to build a caring climate in classrooms and the school as a whole.
- Address and make clear that cruel treatment, including the use of put-downs and ostracizing or purposefully leaving other students out during work and play, is not tolerated. Students need to be encouraged to include all of their peers in kind ways. Preventing these low levels of aggression or precursors to more dangerous forms of violence will help prevent students becoming at greater risk.
- Work to build protective factors for students at high risk, including helping all students develop healthy bonds with school, and have healthy beliefs and clear standards in and about school.
- Create caring, mentoring relationships with all students and be poised to get special help for students at risk.
- Involve at-risk students in the school through cocurricular and academic activities (tutoring, school programs, etc.).
- Build academic skills of all students with careful focus on early literacy skills. Literacy is the foundation of academic success. Many at-risk students need to build their basic literacy or other academic skills, but are reluctant to admit needing help.
- Be on the lookout for bullying (direct and indirect), sexual harassment, child abuse, relational aggression, and relationship/dating violence.

ACTIVITY AND DISCUSSION

For teachers or administrators, it is important to begin to brainstorm what you want to better understand students' perspectives of violence.

Creating questions for interviews or focus groups, deciding how and where to observe students, creating informal questions for surveys, choosing a formal survey, or determining how to identify students' risk and protective factors involves some planning. In collaboration with your colleagues, decide what you want to know about your students' experiences with and perceptions of violence in their lives. These are some guiding questions to start. Your answers will help you develop surveys and questions for interviews and focus groups.

- What do they consider violent?
- What do they report? What goes unreported?
- What are they most afraid of related to violence?
- What are some extreme examples of violence?
- What do students do to keep themselves safe? Is safety something they think about on a regular basis?
- In what ways do you or do others in your school work to build protective factors for students at risk?
- How can we identify problem behaviors that are underreported, such as child abuse, bullying, ostracizing, relational aggression, intimate partner aggression, and sexual harassment?

In addition, consider:

- What structures are in place to identify students at risk using at-risk behavior lists and warning signs included throughout this chapter?
- What structures do we have in place for students at high risk of violence? For students who have been victims of child abuse in the home?
- What structures help us identify and improve protective factors for students at risk?

3

STEP 3 OF THE PEACE
APPROACH: ADVOCATE

Now that you have examined students' perspectives and needs and your own personal perspectives of violence, you are in a better position to advocate for your students' needs. However, before choosing the right program or components of programs to meet your students' needs, you must educate yourself about programs with demonstrated success and the components of programs that might best suit your students' needs. Much research has been done during the past decade to determine which programs in violence prevention and intervention have had demonstrated success in the schools.

Some research projects of programs with demonstrated success have been summarized by the following federal agencies that commissioned groups to review promising and demonstrated programs. The programs have been summarized on the individual agencies' websites.

- The Office of Juvenile Justice and Delinquency Prevention (OJJDP, see http://ojjdp.ncjrs.org)
- The Hamilton Fish National Institute on School and Community Violence (www.hamfish.org)
- The Safe and Drug-Free Schools Programs (www.sdfs.org)
- The National Institutes of Health (www.nih.gov)

These groups have conducted national research projects to determine effective approaches to school violence prevention and intervention. As a teacher or administrator, you can incorporate components of these successful violence prevention programs, such as:

- Developing positive discipline strategies in your classrooms
- Teaching social skills
- Creating caring, cooperative classrooms
- Teaching anger management, either infused in your traditional curriculum or as stand-alone programs
- Teaching conflict resolution skills, either infused in your traditional curriculum or as stand-alone programs
- Working collaboratively with all the people in the school, such as bus drivers, cafeteria workers, librarians, counselors, teachers, administrators, students, janitors, and so on, to create schoolwide approaches to violence prevention

This chapter provides a list of successful programs and offers some suggestions, lists, and places to go for more information. It is important to keep in mind that programs with demonstrated success have had their success within a given context, and may not necessarily have the same success at your school. In addition, not all programs are appropriate for all schools; finding the right program or components based on identified needs is critical to success.

EDUCATING YOURSELF: WHAT WORKS

Derzon and Wilson (1999) classified violence prevention and intervention programs into the following types or categories:

- Administrative techniques (e.g., classroom behavior management, securing the school building/physical facility, creating schoolwide norms for behavior)
- Alternative education/programs (e.g., having places for students who do not respond to conventional means to go)
- Peer mentoring programs

- Personal growth/therapeutic programs
- Self-control (emotions/anger management)
- Social skills training (conflict resolution, interpersonal/relationship/ dating violence prevention)
- Peer mediation
- Educational/instructional programs (e.g., DARE, other programs giving factual information)
- Multifaceted programs (combining three or more of the above strategies)

Programs designed to prevent or reduce violence in schools usually fall in one of the above categories. Based on the data you collected when examining students' needs, you might want to figure out the category or categories on which you would like to focus. This chapter examines and explains many of the successful programs.

Within the classroom, teaching social skills and self-control, such as anger management and conflict resolution skills, can be effective. There is evidence that simply preventing put-downs will reduce violence (Williams 2001). Thus, as teachers or administrators, remaining vigilant over student behavior is essential; even behaviors that once seemed insignificant (bullying, teasing, and put-downs) are important and should not go unnoticed.

National Institute of Justice Report

The National Institute of Justice reported on programs that had demonstrated success in violence prevention (Sherman et al. 1998). They argued the following programs were successful for the following populations (quoted, with additional clarification):

- For infants: Frequent home visits by nurses and other professionals
- For preschoolers: Classes with weekly home visits by preschool teachers
- For delinquent and at-risk youth: Family therapy and parent training
- For schools: Organizational development for innovation
  - Communication and reinforcement of clear consistent norms (such as classroom management and discipline planning)

○ Teaching social competency skills (such as skillstreaming or prosocial skills training—skills-based training strategies that teach students positive behaviors and social skills), anger management, or curricular infusion of skills

The clear message here is that different programs work better with different developmental levels. When advocating for the needs of your students, make sure the components you choose based on their needs are developmentally most appropriate.

The National School Safety Center Report

The National School Safety Center (1998) offered the following steps for preventing or reducing violence in schools (quoted, with some elaboration added for assistance and emphasis):

- Create awareness: Is there violence? What is the nature of it? Who is behaving violently?
- Perform an assessment—surveys, focus groups, observations, etc.
- Use a comprehensive/schoolwide approach [see the checklist at the end of chapter 4].
- Encourage curricular intervention (teaching prosocial skills and conflict resolution in the curriculum).
- Offer conflict resolution training and services.
- Analyze: Is there a plan to control and monitor access to your school?
- Establish disciplinary standards that are clearly communicated to staff, parents, and students and that are enforced fairly and consistently.
- Create consistent discipline plans that are visible, monitored, known, and practiced.
- Address gang activity. Is there a plan to discourage gang activity? Are parents provided information about signs of gang involvement? Are there alternatives to gangs for students?
- Do students have caring adults whom they may approach in crisis situations?
- Prevent weapon concealment.

- Are periodic searches conducted to locate and confiscate weapons? Are other strategies implemented that make it difficult for students to conceal weapons? Are there strict and consistent policies for students caught with weapons?
- Institute alternative education programs.
- Are students suspended for violent acts required to attend alternative educational programs that teach nonviolence?
- Is there a prevention and response plan? Is there a team that can ensure its implementation?
- Is there a strategy to address the needs of students at high risk of becoming serious and violent juvenile offenders? Are appropriate services offered to them (e.g., case management, family therapy, mentoring, tutoring, skills training, etc.)?
- Is there a crisis response plan? (See "Early Warning, Timely Response: A Guide to Safe Schools" at www.air-dc.org/cecp.)

Safe and Drug-Free Schools Expert Panel Report

The Safe and Drug-Free Schools program created an expert panel in 1999–2000 to apply rigorous criteria to identifying school programs that were promising in their ability to prevent violence. The panel also created a list of nine exemplary programs that had demonstrated success based on their criteria. Tables 3.1 and 3.2 have information about the promising and exemplary programs.

However, a word of caution here: the tendency is to buy programs that have had demonstrated success in one school or even multiple schools. Programs are much more effective when they are tailored to meet the needs of your particular school, based on data you find. Be careful not to use these lists simply to buy programs. Use components that meet your school's needs.

Hamilton Fish National Institute on School and Community Violence Report

A number of programs have had demonstrated success in reducing or preventing adolescent violence (summarized in a program paper entitled "Effective Violence Prevention Programs" prepared by the Hamilton Fish

**Table 3.1. Safe, Disciplined, and Drug-Free Schools Expert Panel
Promising Programs (2001)**

Aggression Replacement Training
Arnold P. Goldstein
Professor Emeritus of Education and
Psychology, and Director, Center for
  Research on Aggression
Syracuse University
805 South Crouse Avenue
Syracuse NY 13244
Phone: (315) 443-9641
Fax: (315) 443-5732

**Aggressors, Victims, and Bystanders:
  Thinking and Acting to Prevent
  Violence**
Erica Macheca
Center for School Health Program
Education Development Center, Inc.
55 Chapel Street
Newton MA 02458
Phone: (617) 969-7100
Fax: (617) 244-3436
E-mail: emacheca@edc.org
http://www2.edc.org/thtm/

Al's Pals: Kids Making Healthy Choices
Susan R. Geller, President
Wingspan, LLC
P. O. Box 29070
Richmond VA 23242
Phone: (804) 754-0100
Fax: (804) 754-0200
E-mail: sgeller@wingspanworks.com
http://www.wingspanworks.com

All Stars (Core Program)
William B. Hansen, Ph.D.
Tanglewood Research, Inc.
7017 Albert Pick Road, Suite D
Greensboro NC 27409
Phone: (336) 662-0090
Fax: (336) 662-0099
E-mail: billhansen@tanglewood.net
http://www.tanglewood.net

Child Development Project
Dr. Eric Schaps, President
Developmental Studies Center
2000 Embarcadero, Suite 305
Oakland CA 94606-5300
Phone: (510) 533-0213
Fax: (510) 464-3670

E-mail: Eric_Schaps@devstu.org
http://www.devstu.org

Community of Caring
Brian J. Mooney
Community of Caring, Inc.
1325 G Street NW, Suite 500
Washington DC 20005
Phone: (202) 824-0351
Fax: (202) 824-0351
E-mail: contact@communityofcaring.org
http://www.communityofcaring.org

Creating Lasting Family Connections
Ted N. Strader, Executive Director
Council on Prevention & Education:
  Substances, Inc. (COPES)
845 Barret Avenue
Louisville KY 40204
Phone: (502) 583-6820
Fax: (502) 583-6832
E-mail: tstrader@sprynet.com
http://www.copes.org

Facing History and Ourselves
Terry Tollefson, Ed.D.
Director of Human Resources and
  Evaluation
Facing History and Ourselves National
  Foundation, Inc.
16 Hurd Road
Brookline MA 02445
Phone: (617) 232-1595
Fax: (617) 232-0281
E-mail: Terry_Tollefson@facing.org
http://www.facing.org

Growing Healthy
Director of Education
National Center for Health Education
72 Spring Street, Suite 208
New York NY 10012-4019
Phone: (212) 334-9470
Fax: (212) 334-9845
E-mail: nche@nche.org
http://www.nche.org

I Can Problem Solve (ICPS)
Dr. Myrna B. Shure, Professor
MCP Hahnemann University

Department of Clinical
and Health Psychology
245 N. 15th St. MS 626
Philadelphia PA 19102-1192
Phone: (215) 762-7205
Fax: (215) 762-8625
E-mail: mshure@drexel.edu
http://www.researchpress.com

**Let Each One Touch One
Mentor Program**
Vicki Tomlin, Ph.D.
Denver Public Schools
4051 S. Wabash St.
Denver CO 80237
Phone: (303) 796-0414
Fax: (303) 796-8071
E-mail: vtomlin@dnvr.uswest.net

**Linking the Interests of Families and
Teachers (LIFT)**
Dr. J. Mark Eddy, Researcher
Oregon Social Learning Center
160 East 4th Avenue
Eugene OR 97401
Phone: (541) 485-2711
Fax: (541) 485-7087
E-mail: marke@oslc.org
http://www.oslc.org

Lions-Quest Skills for Adolescence
Greg Long
Quest International
1984 Coffman Road
Newark OH 43055
Phone: (740) 522-6400
Fax: (740) 522-6580
E-mail: gregl@quest.edu
http://www.quest.edu

Lions-Quest Working Toward Peace
Greg Long
Quest International
1984 Coffman Road
Newark OH 43055
Phone: (740) 522-6400
Fax: (740) 522-6580
E-mail: mailto:gregl@quest.edu
http://www.quest.edu

**Michigan Model for Comprehensive
School Health Education**
Don Sweeney
Michigan Department of Community Health,
School Health Unit
3423 N. Martin Luther King Blvd.
Lansing MI 48909
Phone: (517) 335-8390
Fax: (517) 335-8391
E-mail: sweeneyd@state.mi.us
http://www.emc.cmich.edu

**Minnesota Smoking Prevention
Program**
Ann Standing
Hazelden Information and Educational
Services
15251 Pleasant Valley Road
P. O. Box 176
Center City MN 55012
Phone: (800) 328-9000 Ext: 4030
Fax: (651) 213-4577
E-mail: astanding@hazelden.org
http://hazelden.org

Open Circle Curriculum
Pamela Seigle, Executive Director
Reach Out to Schools: Social Competency
Program
The Stone Center, Wellesley Centers for
Women
Wellesley College
106 Central Street
Wellesley MA 02481-8203
Phone: (781) 283-3778
Fax: (781) 283-3717
E-mail: pseigle@wellesley.edu
http://www.wellesley.edu/opencircle

**PATHS Curriculum
(Promoting Alternative Thinking
Strategies)**
Carol A. Kusche, Ph.D.
PATHS Training, LLC
927 10th Avenue East
Seattle WA 98102
Phone: (206) 323-6688
Fax: (206) 323-6688
E-mail: ckusche@attglobal.net
http://www.prevention.psu.edu/PATHS or
http://drp.org

continued

PeaceBuilders
Michael I. Krupnick, President
Heartsprings, Inc.
P.O. Box 12158
Tucson AZ 85732
Phone: (520) 322-9977 (877) 4-PEACE-NOW
Fax: (520) 322-9983
E-mail: mik@heartsprings.org

Peacemakers Program: Violence Prevention for Students in Grades Four through Eight
Jeremy P. Shapiro, Ph.D.
Applewood Centers, Inc.
2525 East 22nd Street
Cleveland OH 44115
Phone: (216) 696-5800 Ext: 1144
Fax: (216) 696-6592
E-mail: jeremyshapiro@yahoo.com

Peers Making Peace
Susan Armoni, Executive Director
PeaceMakers Unlimited, Inc.
2095 N. Collins Blvd., Suite 101
Richardson TX 75080
Phone: (972) 671-9550
Fax: (972) 671-9549
E-mail: Susan.Armoni@pmuinc.com
http://www.pmuinc.com

Positive Action Program
Dr. Carol Gerber Allred
Positive Action, Inc.
264 Fourth Avenue South
Twin Falls ID 83301
Phone: (208) 733-1328 (800) 345-2974
Fax: (208) 733-1590
E-mail: paction@micron.net
http://www.positiveaction.net

Preparing for the Drug-Free Years (PDFY)
Dan Chadrow
Developmental Research and Programs, Inc.
130 Nickerson St., Suite 107
Seattle WA 98109
Phone: (800) 736-2630 Ext: 162
Fax: (206) 736-2630
E-mail: moreinfo@drp.org
http://www.drp.org

Primary Mental Health Project
Deborah B. Johnson
Children's Institute
274 N. Goodman, Suite D103
Rochester NY 14607
Phone: (716) 295-1000 (877) 888-7647
Fax: (716) 295-1090
E-mail: djohnson@childrensinstitute.net
http://www.pmhp.org
or http://www.childrensinstitute.net

Project STAR
Karen Bernstein
University of Southern California
Norris Comprehensive Cancer Center
1441 Eastlake Avenue, Room 3415
Los Angeles CA 90089-9175
Phone: (323) 865-0325
Fax: (323) 865-0134
E-mail: karenber@usc.edu

Responding in Peaceful and Positive Ways (RIPP)
Melanie McCarthy
Youth Violence Prevention Project
Virginia Commonwealth University
808 W. Franklin Street, Box 2018
Richmond VA 23284-2018
Phone: (804) 828-8793
Fax: (804) 827-1511
E-mail: mkmccart@saturn.vcu.edu
http://www.wkap.nl/book.htm/0-306-46386-5

Say It Straight Training
Paula Englander-Golden, Ph.D.
Professor and Director
University of North Texas
Department of Rehabilitation, Social Work and Addictions, Institute for Studies in Addictions
P.O. Box 310919
Denton TX 76203-0919
Phone: (940) 565-3290
Fax: (940) 565-3960
E-mail: golden@scs.cmm.unt.ed or golden@unt.edu

SCARE Program
D. Scott Herrmann, Ph.D.
Tripler Army Medical Center/Child

Psychology Services
One Jarrett White Road
TAMC Hawaii 96859-5000
Phone: (808) 433-2738
Fax: (808) 433-1801
E-mail: don.herrmann@haw.tamc.
amedd.army.mil

Seattle Social Development Project
Development Research and
Programs, Inc.
130 Nickerson Street, Suite 107
Seattle WA 98109
Phone: (206) 286-1805
Fax: (206) 286-1462
E-mail: moreinfo@drp.org
http://www.drp.org

SMART Team
(Students Managing Anger &
Resolution Together)
Kris Bosworth, Ph.D.
Smith Endowed Chair in
Substance Abuse Education
The University of Arizona
Department of Educational Leadership
Smith Prevention Initiatives
College of Education
P.O. Box 210069
Tucson AZ 85721-0069
Phone: (520) 626-4964
Fax: (520) 626-6005
E-mail: boswortk@u.arizona.edu
http://www.drugstats.org

Social Decision Making/Problem
Solving
Linda Bruene-Butler
The University of Medicine and
Dentistry, University Behavioral Health Care
Institute for Quality Research and Training
335 George Street
New Brunswick NJ 08901
Phone: (800) 642-7762
Fax: (732) 235-9277
E-mail: SPSWEB@UMDNJ.EDU
http://www2.umdnj.edu/spsweb/news.htm

Teenage Health Teaching Modules
Erica Macheca
Center for School Health Programs
Education Development Center, Inc.
55 Chapel Street
Newton MA 02458
Phone: (617) 969-7100
Fax: (617) 244-3436
E-mail: emacheca@edc.org
http://www.edc.org/thtm

The Think Time Strategy
J. Ron Nelson, Ph.D.
Research Professor
University of Nebraska, Lincoln
Center for At-Risk Children Services
Barkley Center
Lincoln NE 68583-0738
Phone: (402) 472-0283
Fax: (402) 472-7697
E-mail: rnelson8@unl.edu

Available online at:
www.ed.gov/offices/OERI/ORAD/KAD/expert_panel/2001promising_sddfs.html

Table 3.2.   Safe, Disciplined, and Drug-Free Schools Expert Panel
Exemplary Programs (2001)

Athletes Training and Learning to
Avoid Steroids (ATLAS)
Linn Goldberg, M.D.
Professor of Medicine and Principal
Investigator for the ATLAS Program
Oregon Health Sciences University
ATLAS Program
3181 SW Sam Jackson Park Road (CR 110)
Portland OR 97201
Phone: (503) 494-6559
Fax: (503) 494-1310

E-mail: goldberl@ohsu.ed
http://www.ohsu.edu/som-hpsm/info.htm

CASASTART
Lawrence F. Murray CSW
Senior Program Associate
The National Center on Addiction and
Substance Abuse at
Columbia University (CASA)
633 Third Avenue, 19th Floor
New York NY 10017

continued

Table 3.2.   Safe, Disciplined, and Drug-Free Schools Expert Panel Exemplary Programs (2001) (*continued*)

Phone: (212) 841-5208
Fax: (212) 956-8020
E-mail: lmurray@casacolumbia.org
http://www.casacolumbia.org

Life Skills Training
National Health Promotion Associates, Inc.
141 South Central Avenue, Suite 208
Hartsdale NY 10530
Phone: (914) 421-2525
Fax: (914) 683-6998
E-mail: training@nhpanet.com
http://www.lifeskillstraining.com

OSLC Treatment Foster Care
Patricia Chamberlain, Executive Director
Oregon Social Learning Center Community
    Programs
160 East 4th Avenue
Eugene OR 97401
Phone: (541) 485-2711
Fax: (541) 485-7087
E-mail: pattic@oslc.org
http://oslc.org

Project ALERT
G. Bridget Ryan
725 S. Figueroa St., Suite 1615
Los Angeles CA 90017
Phone: (800) 253-7810
Fax: (213) 623-0585
E-mail: info@projectalert.best.org
http://www.projectalert.best.org

**Project Northland- Alcohol Prevention
    Curriculum**
Ann Standing
Hazelden Information and Educational
    Services
15251 Pleasant Valley Road
PO Box 176

Center City MN 55012
Phone: (800) 328-9000 Ext: 4030
Fax: (651) 213-4577
E-mail: astanding@hazelden.org
http://www.hazelden.org

**Project T.N.T.-Towards No Tobacco
    Use**
Sue Wald
ETR Associates (Education, Training, &
    Research Associates)
4 Carbonero Way
Scotts Valley CA 95066
Phone: (831) 438-4060 Ext: 164
Fax: (831) 438-4284
E-mail: wals@etr.org
http://www.etr.org

**Second Step: A Violence Prevention
    Curriculum**
Committee for Children
Client Support Services Department
2203 Airport Way South, Suite 500
Seattle WA 98134
Phone: (206) 343-1223 (800) 634-4449
Fax: (206) 343-1445
E-mail: info@cfchildren.org
http://www.cfchildren.org

**Strengthening Families Program:
    For Parents and Youth 10-14**
Virginia Molgaard
Institute for Social and Behavioral Research
2625 N. Loop, Suite 500
Iowa State University
Ames IA 50010
Phone: (515) 294-8762
Fax: (515) 294-3613
E-mail: vmolgaar@iastate.edu
http://www.extens

Available online at:
www.ed.gov/offices/OERI/ORAD/KAD/expert_panel/2001exemplary_sddfs.html
Reprinted from the U.S. Department of Education.

National Institute on School and Community Violence, 2000). These programs are based on a complicated metaanalysis procedure to determine their effectiveness. A full description is available at the website. A summary of the programs with demonstrated success based on their criteria is shown in table 3.3.

Table 3.3. Results from the Hamilton Fish National Institute on School and Community Violence's Metaanalysis of Programs with Demonstrated Success

The Anger Coping Program (middle and early secondary school program)
Contact information:
John Lochman, Ph.D.
Department of Psychology
University of Alabama
Box 870348
Tuscaloosa AL 35487
Tel: (205) 348-5083
Fax: (205) 348-8648
E-mail: jlochman@gp.as.ua.edu

The Brainpower Program (late elementary program)
Contact information:
Cynthia Hudley, Ph.D.
Graduate School of Education
University of California at Santa Barbara
2210 Phelps Hall UCSB
Santa Barbara CA 93106-9490
Tel: (805) 893-8324
Fax: (805) 893-7264
E-mail: hudley@education.ucsb.edu

The First Step to Success Program (kindergarten program)
Ordering Information
Sopris West
4093 Specialty Place
Longmont CO 80504
Tel: (800) 547-6747
Fax: (303) 776-5934
www.sopriswest.com

Good Behavior Game (early elementary program)
Contact information:
Sheppard G. Kellam

Department of Mental Hygiene
Johns Hopkins University School of Hygiene and Public Health
Prevention Research Center
Mason F. Lord Building, Suite 500
5200 Eastern Avenue
Baltimore MD 21224
Tel: (410) 550-3445

I Can Problem Solve (elementary school program)
Contact information:
Myrna Shure, Ph.D.
MCP Hahnemann University
245 N. 15th Street
MS 626
Philadelphia PA 19102
Tel: (215) 762-7205
E-mail: mshure@drexel.edu

Kid Power Program (elementary school program)
Contact information:
Mike Bennett
River Region Human Services, Inc.
330 West State Street
Jacksonville FL 32202
Tel: (904) 359-6571, ext. 135
Fax: (904) 359-6583
E-mail: rrhsmike@msn.com

Metropolitan Child Area Study (violence and substance abuse, adolescents)
Contact information:
Patrick H. Tolan, Ph.D.
Institute for Juvenile Research
Department of Psychiatry

continued

Table 3.3.   Results from the Hamilton Fish National Institute on School and Community Violence's Metaanalysis of Programs with Demonstrated Success (continued)

University of Illinois at Chicago
Chicago IL 60612
Tel: (312) 413-1893
Fax: (312) 413-1703
E-mail: Tolan@uic.edu

Peer Mediation Program
Contact information:
Donna Crawford, Executive Director
National Center for Conflict Resolution
  Education
110 West Main Street
Urbana IL 61801
Tel: (217) 384-4118
Fax: (217) 384-4322
E-mail: crawford@nccre.org
www.nccre.org

Positive Adolescent Choices Training (PACT)
Contact information:
Betty R. Yung, Ph.D.
School of Professional Psychology
Wright State University
Ellis Human Development Institute
9 N. Edwin C. Moses Boulevard
Dayton OH 45407
Tel: (937) 775-4300
Fax: (937) 775-4323
E-mail: betty.yung@wright.edu

Teaching Students to Be Peacemakers
Contact information:
Linda Johnson
Interaction Book Company
7208 Cornelia Drive

Edina MN 55435
Tel: (612) 831-7060
Fax: (612) 831-9332

Tools for Effective Violence Prevention: School Security
For more information, contact:
Kenneth S. Trump, President and CEO
National School Safety and Security Services
Corporate Headquarters
P.O. Box 110123
Cleveland OH 44111-2950
Tel: (216) 251-3067
Fax: (216) 251-4417
KENTRUMP@aol.com
www.schoolsecurity.org

Think First (for secondary school students)
Contact information:
Jim Larson, Ph.D.
Coordinator, School Psychology Program
Department of Psychology
University of Wisconsin - Whitewater
Whitewater WI 53190
Tel: (414) 472-5412
Fax: (414) 472-1863

Violence Prevention Curriculum for Adolescents
Contact information:
Education Development Center, Inc.
55 Chapel Street
Newton MA 02458-1060
Tel: (800) 225-4276
www.edc.org

More information is available about these programs and others at the Hamilton Fish National Institute on School and Community Violence website. For a full text copy of this program report, go to the website at http://hamfish.org/pub/evpp.html.

There are some elements that promising and exemplary programs have in common: social skills training (including communication, negotiation, listening, composure), self-awareness/evaluation and reflection of violence, empathy training, problem solving, anger management, and conflict resolution. The intervention at the alternative school for weapons expulsion (WANTS) focused on teaching these skills, pulling from a variety of these intervention components. For a summary and description of these skills, see table 3.4 later in the chapter.

What can you do as a teacher or administrator?

- Educate yourself about social skills training, conflict resolution, anger management, and other components of successful programs.
- Educate yourself about other issues your students face: gang membership and drug use and abuse, relational violence, emotional or physical cruelty.
- Think about ways you can infuse these strategies into your classroom and curriculum (collaborating with others about strategies for this).
- Allow students a safe place to practice their skills. Consider certain classrooms where collaboration and conflict resolution skills are vital to one's success and a skilled teacher is committed to allowing students to practice.
- Use data you collect to drive the choices you make about what strategies to implement.
- Have a strategy for holding people accountable to the fidelity of whatever program or components of programs you choose to implement (e.g., hiring someone whose job it is to oversee the implementation, bonuses for demonstrated success).

As described above, there are many common elements of successful programs in school violence prevention. As you begin to advocate on behalf of your students' needs, you will need to collaborate with other teachers, parents, administrators, and staff to create schoolwide approaches to violence prevention. But, you may be wondering, what options do I have as a teacher that I can implement in my own classrooms? There are some skills you can learn and there are strategies for imparting skills to your students. The important message, however, is that it is difficult for your classroom to be an island in an otherwise dangerous and threatening sea. This is why collaboration and schoolwide approaches are essential to the success of programs.

Nevertheless, if you are focusing on your own classroom as a part of a schoolwide approach or as an island, skills can be taught in your classroom. Conflict resolution, anger management infusion, parental involvement, and consistent discipline are all approaches you can learn more about and build into your classroom.

SOCIAL SKILLS TRAINING

Social skills training involves teaching students the skills that many adults take for granted: starting a conversation, negotiation, refusal skills, communication (verbal and nonverbal), saying thank you, and so on. Some programs with demonstrated success, such as Goldstein and McGinnis's (1997) "Skillstreaming the Adolescent" or "Elementary Student" or Goldstein's "Aggression Replacement Training" (listed in table 3.1) and other programs, engage students in role-plays of realistic situations (that students themselves identify) where they employ these social skills.

You may want to think about the social skills your students may need some help with (be careful to be developmentally appropriate), and plan some strategies for building these into your classroom curriculum. Some of the references at the end of the book will provide some guidance.

CHARACTER EDUCATION

Some of these social skills may also be addressed in character education curricula. Character education has received much attention. For example, New York State's recent (2000) SAVE (Schools Against Violence Everywhere) legislation mandates that all public schools in the state will have a character education program in place. Teaching students the "golden rule" of treating others as you want to be treated yourself can often be a part of such character education programs.

Character education can be infused into the classroom and curricula along with social skills. Many argue that character education is an essential part of violence prevention in schools.

The character traits included in most character education programs are:

- Responsibility: Accountability for one's words and actions; fulfilling tasks with reliability, dependability, and commitment.
- Perseverance: Pursuing positive goals with determination and patience, and with fortitude when confronted with failure.
- Caring: Treating others with kindness, compassion, generosity, and a forgiving spirit. Nel Noddings (1992) describes the importance of care in schools and how schools must create a culture and teach caring.
- Self-discipline: Controlling emotions, words, actions, impulses, and desires; always trying your hardest. Anger management programs focus on self-control, composure, and identifying one's cues, triggers, and reducers.
- Citizenship: Obeying the law and giving to your school, community, and country. Programs such as "Judicious Discipline" by Forrest Gathercoal demonstrate strategies teachers can use in the classroom to design classroom rules around the U.S. Constitution. Students learn citizenship and take an active role in the rules of their classroom.
- Honesty: Telling the truth, admitting wrongdoing, being trustworthy and having integrity.
- Courage: Standing up for and doing the right thing, even when things are difficult and even when it means not following the crowd.
- Fairness: Behaving justly and promoting equity and equality; cooperation with one another; recognizing the uniqueness and value of each individual within our diverse society.
- Respect: Demonstrating a high regard for authority, other people, self, and country; treating others as you would want to be treated (the "golden rule"); understanding that all people have value as human beings. (List reprinted from www.charactered.net, with additions from the author.)

Helping children define character and the kinds of character traits they wish to possess themselves is part of character education. Often empathy (understanding another person's feelings) is part of character education programs as well. Empathy training has been found to have some success in preventing violence in schools. Helping children to respect and appreciate another's perspective is critical in preventing children from physically or verbally harming one another. Internalizing the basic tenets of character education is also important.

CONFLICT RESOLUTION

Many schools today recognize the importance of conflict resolution, have established mediation programs, and have taught students and teachers or administrators conflict resolution skills. Some resources about conflict resolution are provided in the reference section. There are also experts in most communities who provide training in the peaceful resolution of conflict.

Conflict resolution involves communication and the creation of a peaceful resolution to conflict. Generally, when two people are in a conflict, both have a great deal of energy. The one who is trained or best able to lower the other's anger by actively listening and reflecting what the other is saying attempts to lower the anger so that the two can engage in problem solving to come up with a win-win solution to the conflict. There must be a culture of respect and caring for this kind of conflict resolution to happen. Also, students must be trained in how to be active listeners and problem solvers.

Active/Reflective Listening and Using Open-Ended Questions

Active or reflective listening involves one party reflecting back what he or she hears the other party saying in a way that is nonthreatening, honest, and caring. It is a way of checking in to see if the listener is hearing the other person correctly. If done well, both parties feel respected and can calm down. Open-ended questions also allow the person who is most angry to unload some of their anger and allow the other person to figure out what is wrong.

Angry statement: "I can't believe you totally trashed my new CD I loaned you!"

Reflective statement (reflecting content and mood) and open-ended question: "I can see you are upset about your CD. What happened?"

Response (a bit calmer): "Well, yeah. What did you do to it? I got home and played it and it was skipping all over the place!"

Reflective statement: "So it was skipping through the whole disk and you thought I did that when I borrowed it?"

If the reflective student was not able to remain calm, and said, "I didn't do it, you liar!" this might be a good case to refer to mediation where a neutral third party can help both parties have their cases heard and negotiate a mutually beneficial solution.

Using "I" Statements

When engaged in a conflict, constantly blaming the other, "you did this" or "you did that," usually results in more anger and conflict. Using "I" statements helps. "I felt really upset when I didn't hear from you." Or, "I was really hurt when I wasn't invited to your party." Teaching students to use "I" statements is good practice for teaching personal responsibility over one's emotions rather than blaming others for our feelings.

Conflict resolution is an empowering way for students to learn how to resolve their own conflicts nonviolently. However, sometimes it is necessary to have some outside assistance.

PEER MEDIATION

When both parties are too upset to engage in active listening or problem solving by themselves, a referral to mediation is sometimes a positive strategy. A third party who has been trained to be neutral and respectful of both sides can often help those in conflict come to a peaceful solution. In peer mediation programs, the third party is a trained peer. In regular mediation programs, the neutral party may be an adult in the school. Generally, peer mediation follows a structure similar to the one Wolowiec (1994, 16) from the American Bar Association outlines.

- Part I. Introduction
  1. Have participants introduce themselves.
  2. Explain the mediator's role.

3. Explain the ground rules. An example of a good ground rule is: Respect each other.
4. Explain steps of mediation.
5. Ask for any questions before you begin.
- Part II. Telling the Story
  1. Both parties tell their side of the story to the mediator— uninterrupted, with each getting a chance to speak as much as he or she wants.
  2. Summarize both parties' side of the story.
  3. Make sure you understand the conflict.
  4. Make sure the parties understand the conflict.
- Part III. Identifying Facts and Feelings
  1. Each party tells his or her side of the story to the other.
  2. Bring out facts and feelings of what the parties say.
  3. Have parties change roles.
  4. Summarize the facts and feelings of both sides.
- Part IV. Generating Options
  1. Ask both parties how they can solve the problem.
  2. Write down all possible solutions.
  3. Check off only the solution(s) that both parties can agree to.
- Part V. Agreement
  1. Use only the solutions that both parties agree to.
  2. Write the contract up in parties' own words.
  3. Everybody signs it.
- Part VI. Follow-Up
  1. Explain how follow-up works.
  2. Remember to thank the people for being there and for letting the mediation service help them.

I have seen both peer mediation and regular mediation programs work successfully with even the most angry and hostile children and adolescents. There are times, however, when mediation may be inappropriate. First, parties in conflict should have a cooling-off period. Second, the mediator needs to be able to be neutral (having no social or academic relationship with the parties); sometimes I have seen peer mediations involve two peer mediators. Third, sexual harassment cases are inappropriate for mediation (I have seen mediation used to resolve these ineffectively). Ideally, everyone in the school knows what mediation is so that appropriate referrals are made. Peer mediation is most successful in cultures where mediation is seen as an attractive, viable option. All staff knows what peer mediation is and the nature of appropriate cases. Students even self-refer because they can recognize when they need a third party to assist them in resolving their conflict.

In addition, as a teacher or administrator, you may infuse conflict resolution skills such as problem solving and active/reflective listening into your curriculum. You could discuss conflicts within readings in language arts classes and ways they were resolved, peacefully or not. You may also find conflicts or wars within social studies and discuss how they might have been resolved peacefully. More strategies for infusion will be discussed in the next section.

ANGER MANAGEMENT TRAINING AND INFUSION

Teaching students how to manage anger is critical to violence prevention. One of the first steps in teaching students how to deal with their anger is to teach them to recognize triggers, cues, and reducers.

- Anger *triggers* are those events or situations that make us angry (examples include being yelled at, being called a mean name, etc.)
- *Cues* are the physiological feelings we feel when we are getting angry (examples include feeling sweaty, stomachache, nausea, shaking, etc.)
- *Reducers* are the things we can do to make ourselves feel better when we are angry (examples include exercise, deep breaths, walking away, etc.)

It is important to remember that not all anger leads to violence, so it is important to help students see the link and figure out ways they can prevent anger from turning violent.

Learning these skills can be done as a stand-alone lesson and reinforced within your traditional curriculum (infused). Some strategies are recommended within the matrix in table 3.4 on how to weave components of anger management and conflict resolution into the traditional curricular areas (mathematics, science, social studies, and language arts).

Table 3.4. Anger Management Competencies and Possible Infusion Strategies

Competencies	Components/Skills	Examples of possible strategies for infusion in subject areas
Knowledge Awareness	Anger awareness - anger triggers (what makes me angry?) - anger cues (how do I know when I'm getting angry?) - anger reducers (what can I do to calm myself when I'm angry or becoming angry?) - anger control reminders (how can I remember these strategies when I'm becoming angry?) - developmental growth factors (what strategies are developmentally appropriate?) Violence awareness - What is violence? Violence definitions? Attitudes and perceptions of violence? How are these different? How are these the same? - What constitutes good versus bad violence - What is the difference between controllable and uncontrollable violence? - What are the links between anger and violence? (e.g., connections, consequences, establishing the need to change)	• *Language Arts*: Reading stories with conflicts or anger and describing cues, triggers, and reducers, and links between anger and violence in stories. Discussions of definitions of violence and links between anger and violence and strategies for preventing violence. • *Science*: What scientific creations began within a culture of conflict (i.e., the earth is flat! Darwinism?) Also, the scientific method (the idea of applying a method to solving a problem), problem solving.
Self-Evaluation/ Assessment/ Reflection	Self-respect Self-awareness and acceptance Self-appraisal Self-reinforcement	
Empathy	Ability to change self (attitudes and behaviors) Increasing sensitivity - awareness of own point of view - awareness of other people's points of view	• *Art*: Perspective taking (photography, video, drawing) Violent images in music and art • *For all*: Collaborative working groups—how to work collaboratively, how to listen effectively, how to recognize when someone is making you angry
Composure	Personal control/Coping strategies* - dealing with anger - dealing with embarrassment - dealing with pressure - techniques to keep calm - relaxation training	*Physical Education*: Using physical activity as an anger reducer, sports importance of remaining calm; recognizing the importance of this

*explore coping strategies for dealing with
grief—many children are dealing with grief
and mask it with anger

Communication	Verbal skills - open-ended questions - paraphrasing/reflecting tone and content - I statements Non-verbal skills - eye contact - body language Negotiation skills - finding commonalities - strategies for finding win-win solutions Listening skills - paraphrasing - summarizing	*Social studies:* Historical conflicts, links with anger and violence and possible avoidance of violence by recognizing anger. Also, ways conflicts might have been resolved peacefully by examining the issues for each side and engaging in creative problem solving.
Problem Solving	1. Awareness of necessary conditions for problem solving (both parties must be calm enough to discuss the problem and able to listen to each other's needs and feelings) 2. Defining the problem 3. Generating how-to statements 4. Brainstorming possible solutions 5. Negotiating 6. Choosing alternatives 7. Considering implications 8. Developing follow-up plans	*Mathematics:* How do we solve problems in mathematics? How can we apply problem-solving techniques within conflict resolution and anger management to these? In what ways can we apply problem-solving techniques to personal conflicts?

Because teachers are such busy people and have so many curricular standards thrust upon them by their districts and states, infusing social skills, conflict resolution, anger management, and other skills into the existing curriculum can prevent add-on programs and time away from instruction. Developing the lesson plans to do this is challenging and takes time, but the rewards can be very powerful. Administrators must make time and provide training, as well as hold teachers accountable for lessons, if infusion is to be a success at your school.

At WANTS, students were taught skills of anger management, social skills, and conflict resolution in an independent class as well as having them infused into their traditional classes. In addition, there were two separate times in which students were encouraged to practice their new skills. The first was a literacy program where students would read to younger children. These skills became very important for students. As one WANTS student told me, he had to stop conflicts that originated between the younger children quite frequently. In addition, students were building their very weak literacy skills.

Second, some WANTS students were involved in an art course during which they needed to practice their new social skills, conflict resolution, collaboration, and anger management. In addition, as a part of their art creations, they often had to engage in perspective taking (being able to see situations from another person's perspective) and building empathy skills as a part of this perspective taking.

Students involved in the art program indicated in surveys and interviews as well as observations that they were more comfortable using the skills, used them more often, and were more likely to use the skills beyond their time at WANTS than those not involved in the art project where they could practice their skills (see Burstyn and Davis 2002).

PARENTAL INVOLVEMENT

As teachers or administrators, you are keenly aware of the important role of parents in supporting what you teach students. Parental involvement is the key to a successful violence prevention program in your school. Parents should have a voice. They can tell you what their issues, frustrations, and fears are, and they can help you advocate for funding to support any programs you might choose.

Parents are busy people. Sometimes it is difficult to get them into school or to reach them on the telephone (if they even have a telephone). Nevertheless, it is important to continue trying to engage parents to make them feel welcome in your classroom and to make sure they know that you value their opinions and thoughts. Often, parents who seem to be unavailable or disengaged from their child's school experiences are those who have had negative school experiences themselves. It becomes essential that you create a supportive place for parents to go in the school, and times when their voices are not only heard but where actions are taken to address their concerns.

Involving Parents at WANTS

WANTS teachers had a difficult time getting parents to come to parent-teacher conferences or even speak to them on the telephone. As it turned out, many parents worked several jobs at night and during the day, had multiple children, and some did not have telephones. Teachers initially had assumed that the parents did not care, but the reality was that they had challenging lives that did not always allow them to take time out to go to school at night or during the day. Struggling to make ends meet, some could not afford telephones. And some were marginally or completely illiterate and unable to respond to written material sent home.

Recognizing these obstacles to getting parents involved, we implemented a family component at WANTS during the 1999–2000 school year based on our work developing the program in 1998–1999. This component involved social work interns who conducted home visits and group meetings. Parents were told about and had the opportunity to experience the communication, anger management, and problem-solving skills being taught to their children in the school. Families were also linked to appropriate service agencies as needed. We also had parent dinners and offered transportation and child care, if needed. The dinners were held in a relaxed atmosphere where parents, teachers, and administrators could get to know each other.

We discovered that parents and guardians (almost exclusively mothers) had struggled with raising their children. Most knew that their children had difficulty in school, but did not know how to make things better. They liked WANTS because of the smaller class sizes and the individualized attention. However, they still had difficulty getting their children to go to school. Mothers also said that they recognized that their children had been aggressive from the time they were very young. They expressed frustration and powerlessness; many wanted help. Home visits are a very powerful tool to get parents invested in their children's education. When parents are invested, their children are more invested, and are more likely to go to school. The quantitative data revealed that children who believe that their parents do not want them to behave violently and that they will get in trouble if they behave violently in school were more likely to use nonaggressive strategies when faced with a conflict (Corvo and Williams 2002).

Parental involvement needs to be an essential component of any successful intervention for working with youth at risk of violence. Figuring out ways to engage parents of troubled youth in positive ways (positive phone calls or notes home, and finding some way to recognize positive achievements of students whose parents are difficult to engage) is critical for the enduring success of programs.

Learning from One Exemplary Parent Program

Among the exemplary programs listed by the Safe and Drug-Free Schools program's expert panel is the "Strengthening Families" program available from Iowa State Extension (www.extension.iastate.edu/sfp/). The program involves content for adolescents as shown in table 3.5.

These topics can be offered as components you may want to implement in a parent program if you feel such a program is necessary to combat violence in your school. You may want to contact the National Parent-Teacher Association at www.pta.org for more information on getting parents more involved in your school.

Table 3.5. Strengthening Families Program Content

Parent Sessions 1–7 Topics	Youth Session 1–7 Topics	Family Sessions 1–7 Topics
• Using Love and Limits • Making House Rules • Encouraging Good Behavior • Using Consequences • Building Bridges • Protecting Against Substance Abuse • Using Community Resources	• Having Goals and Dreams • Appreciating Parents • Dealing with Stress • Following Rules • Handling Peer Pressure I • Handling Peer Pressure II • Reaching Out to Others	• Supporting Goals and Dreams • Appreciating Family Members • Using Family Members • Understanding Family Values • Building Family Communication • Reaching Our Goals • Putting It All Together and Graduation
Parent Boosters 1–4 Topics	**Youth Boosters 1–4 Topics**	**Family Boosters 1–4 Topics**
• Handling Stress • Communicating When You Don't Agree • Reviewing Love and Limits Skills • Reviewing How to Help with Peer Pressure	• Handling Conflict • Making Good Friends • Getting the Message Across • Practicing Our Skills	• Understanding Each Other • Listening to Each Other • Understanding Family Roles • Using Family Strengths

Reprinted from www.extension.iastate.edu/sfp

As teachers or administrators, your best approach is to use a combination of home visits, informal get-togethers around a meal, positive contacts home, and formal programs for parents using components from successful programs as you create a safer school.

DISCIPLINE PLANNING

When I talked with teachers or administrators at WANTS about Forrest Gathercoal's strategy of giving students a voice in developing a code of conduct and learning to balance rights and responsibilities consistent with the amendments to the U.S. constitution (described in his book *Judicious Discipline*), teachers said things such as "These students have no rights—WANTS is punishment for bringing a weapon to school." We struggled to get past this concept to one where students and teachers could have conversations with students about their constitutional rights and how they had lost some of their rights because of their failure to obey the rules of weapon carrying.

Although students struggled with some of the concepts, it went well when teachers tried this strategy in class. After some descriptions of the rights and responsibilities guaranteed by the Constitution, one teacher asked students, "What responsibilities come with your rights?"

One of the students replied, "Don't put yourself in certain positions. Don't put yourself in trouble in school, or they'll move you to WANTS."

The teacher said, "You have the right to wear clothes, but what is your responsibility in school with this right?"

A student said, "No sexy things for the rights of others, but that doesn't leave out baggy clothes."

They continued back and forth and Annie (the teacher) said, "How about health and safety?"

Student: "I have the right to be safe."

Annie: "How would it apply here? Is it more than physical safety?"

Student: "Yeah, it's emotional safety, too, the right not to be picked on for being short."

Annie: "Others?"

Student: "Someone comes in all loud! I have the right to have a peaceful educational classroom. You have the right to express your opinion, but your opinion should not have disses or put-downs."

Conversations that involved teaching students how to live in a democratic society, understanding their rights and responsibilities, and giving them a voice in developing rights and responsibilities consistent with the law of the land yielded fruitful results. Students, particularly WANTS students, often feel disenfranchised and that their voices do not matter. They are not part of the power structure. As Epp and Watkinson (1996, 175) wrote,

> The education system, which is bound by human rights legislation, values and principles, has the same constitutional obligation—that is, to embody respect for the inherent dignity of each student, to commit to equality and social justice, and to adjust the education system to accommodate a wide variety of beliefs and group differences. Democratizing education is a constitutional obligation.

Gathercoal would agree, and has developed strategies for doing what Epp and Watkinson argue schools are obligated to do. *Judicious Discipline* provides a great way to teach the constitution while giving students a voice in discipline planning.

Discipline and Classroom Management

The goals of good classroom discipline include the following:

- Be consistent schoolwide. Have clearly articulated outcomes or responses for specific behaviors (including positive behaviors). Have these outcomes and responses visible and known.
- Be proactive instead of reactive; emphasize positive problem solving and reward children when they engage in the use of prosocial skills instead of reactive punitive responses.
- Recognize and work to eliminate put-downs, ostracizing behaviors, and other mean treatment.
- Have visible and supportive leadership. Visible, engaged, responsive, supportive, and consistent leaders are critical to the success of discipline programs.
- Have staff involvement and commitment. All school staff (including janitors, teaching assistance, librarians, bus drivers, hall and cafeteria monitors, etc.) need to be included and committed to develop, implement, revise, and maintain the discipline plan toward the establishment of a consistent/predictable environment.

- Set high expectations for student behavior. Administration and staff with high academic and social expectations encourage better student performance.
- Know when to refer. There should be clear guidelines for what behavior results in what action so that all students and school personnel know exactly what the results of a given act will be; this should include appropriate definitions/responses to minor infractions, serious infractions, and illegal infractions.
- Create a positive climate. Establish structures that encourage positive social behavior as well as solid academic accomplishments.
- Collaborate with all members of school and appropriate outside agencies that serve youth (i.e., social services, mental health departments, juvenile justice, etc.).
- Set rules that all members of the school body (especially students) are involved in creating and see value in. Make sure these rules are visible, clear, consistently enforced, functional, fair, reviewed, and subject to evaluation and review.
- Monitor and evaluate. Make sure discipline plans are evaluated to determine how well they are working for students and staff. Collect data in the ways discussed in this book (informal and formal) to determine how well these rules are working.

Understanding the Acting-Out Cycle

As teachers or administrators attempting to deal with students' acting-out behavior, it helps to know that there is a clear acting-out cycle that has been identified (Walker, Colvin, and Ramsey 1995).

1. Calm
2. Triggers
3. Agitation
4. Acceleration
5. Peak
6. De-escalation

Working with students to recognize their own cues, triggers, and reducers can be a part of preventive discipline—or stopping the acting-out cycle.

MAKING THE SCHOOL ENVIRONMENT SAFER

The physical environment of the school has an impact on how students think of themselves and their attitude about school as well as their safety. Dilapidated school buildings send a clear message to students that they are not worthy of a clean, new, state-of-the-art school. Poor physical structure, architectural design, lighting, and other issues of the physical layout of a school may cause more violence to occur.

Crowe (1991) wrote a book entitled *Crime Prevention through Environmental Design: Applications of Architectural Design and Space Management Concepts*. The concept of Crime Prevention through Environmental Design (now referred to as CPTED—pronounced sep-ted) has been adapted for schools to create spaces where students and staff feel safer, with improved lighting and better flow of traffic, use of space, and so forth. Schneider (2001, 1), in his article "Safer Schools through Environmental Design," wrote, "A CPTED analysis of a school evaluates crime rates, office-referral data, school cohesiveness and stability, as well as core design shortcomings of the physical environment, such as blind hallways, uncontrolled entries, or abandoned areas that attract problem behavior." He outlined the following core principles of CPTED:

1. Natural surveillance: keeping an eye on the whole environment without taking extraordinary measures to do so. Typical obstacles to natural surveillance include solid walls and lack of windows that provide visibility to areas of the school building that have experienced a high incidence of problem behaviors. Pruning shrubbery is one step that can be taken to improve natural surveillance of school grounds.
2. Natural access control: determining who can or cannot enter a facility. Obstacles to access control include unsupervised, unlocked entrances to the building. Converting several secondary doors into locked, alarmed, emergency exits is one way to improve access control.
3. Territoriality: establishing recognized authority and control over the environment, along with cultivating a sense of belonging. Poor border definition can impede territoriality. Jointly controlled parkland adjacent to a school would be an example of poor border def-

inition. School uniforms offer one approach to both establishing a sense of belonging and making it easy to distinguish between students and nonstudents (2).

The website www.cpted.org has more information, as does the full text of the Schneider (2001) article.

Consider the physical layout of your school and the ways you might improve the physical structure of the school. CPTED specialists are available for consultation to help with design plans and decisions.

INTERVENTION STRATEGIES

Until now, this book has focused on prevention strategies. If prevention efforts are successful, the need for intervention efforts will be reduced. However, it is unlikely that the need for intervention will be completely eliminated. Teachers, administrators, and other school personnel, when asked to discuss issues associated with school violence, often raise issues of gangs and drugs. I include these topics under this discussion of "intervention," as the goals of prevention are to reduce and ultimately eliminate these problems.

Because such problems are so prevalent in schools today, we must address the issues surrounding gangs and drugs in school violence: how to recognize problems, what you should look out for, and what you can do as a teacher when planning violence prevention strategies to address gangs and drugs, as well as how to determine when students pose a real threat.

Understanding Gang Activity

Many people seem to connect gangs and school violence. However, there is school violence without gangs, and there are gang members who may not be violent in schools. Gang membership is a complex phenomenon, and there is much denial among school personnel about gang-related problems.

One school where I conducted my research—a school with much gang involvement—had the superintendent mail a letter to parents that the violence the school was experiencing was "not gang-related." The school district and community used terms such as "street crews" when discussing "gangs." School personnel and community members alike would say things such as "We don't have gangs like the Bloods and the Crips, so these are just wannabes; they're like street crews." The students, on the other hand, knew that these were gangs. There were violent initiations, drug dealing, colors, signs, and violent activities that the gang members were supposed to engage in to demonstrate their loyalty.

Students (boys and girls alike) told me in confidential interviews about the violent initiations. Boys would be beaten by several other young men at a time for a sustained period to be initiated. Girls told me that they had to have sex with multiple partners (be gang-raped), often at the same time, in violent ways, to become a part of a gang.

Students felt that gang membership was essential to their safety. Gangs, the students believed, would protect you and keep you safe. Adults simply told them, gangs are bad and should be avoided. This created quite a conflict. This conflict exists between teachers or administrators and students in gang-infested neighborhoods.

Working with gang-related violence and other issues related to gang membership is challenging because students so often feel membership is a vital part of their own survival.

What you can do as a teacher and administrator:

- Talk to your students about gangs and find out their perceptions of and experiences with gangs.
- Find out which students are hanging around with gang-involved students. These students are at high risk for becoming gang involved.
- Learn to recognize gang symbols, signs, names, and colors. (In schools where gangs are most problematic, most students are pretty open about gang membership with other students, if you listen.)
- Ask students in confidential surveys or interviews about gang involvement and activities (initiations such as "jump-ins" and "sex-ins").
- Encourage students to find alternative strategies for staying safe. Offer attractive alternatives/options to gang involvement that help students stay safe and remain socially involved with friends who are positive role models.
- Collaborate with community agencies to reduce gang problems.

I worked with students who were heavily gang involved at WANTS. I taught them how to read children's books and work as tutors with young children at a local community center. Just this experience of feeling like a mentor and a worthwhile member of society helped them feel more engaged in their learning, and their participation in school improved. They also were involved in fewer violent episodes in school. The same strategies of teaching social skills, conflict resolution, anger management, and mentoring help students involved in gangs as well. However, it is important to recognize that they may have additional safety issues, such as crossing gang territory to get to school (leading to chronic truancy), involvement in the criminal justice system, and involvement in criminal activities other than violence. It is important to better understand the gang problems of your own students.

Understanding Drugs and Their Role in Violence

The role of drugs in violence is complex. Violent acts are more likely to be committed under the influence of certain drugs. Fights, rapes, and other assaults are committed under the influence of alcohol and other drugs the overwhelming majority of the time. Violence is often associated with the criminal world of drug dealing, and violence is associated with the gangs that may be involved with drug sales and use.

Some drugs are more likely to contribute to violence, partly because of their availability and social acceptance and partly because of the nature of the drug itself. Some of the most popular drugs under which much violence occurs are:

Alcohol.   Far and away the most widely accepted, used, and abused drug under which most violence occurs is alcohol. The fact that alcohol is a depressant is intriguing when some become more aggressive and violent under the influence. By reducing inhibitions, individuals under the influence who have a predisposition toward aggressive behavior are more at risk for violence.

Ritalin.   Yes, the drug used to control attention deficit hyperactivity disorder is a stimulant that, when abused by those for whom it is not intended, can lead to aggressive behavior. I include it in this list because it is growing in popularity among school-aged children as a drug of abuse.

Cocaine/Crack.   Cocaine is a stimulant that can be snorted, injected, eaten, or smoked (in the form of crack). Violence not only surrounds the sale of this drug, but the stimulant properties make users sometimes feel stronger and more aggressive. Users may commit violent crimes to obtain the drug or money for the drug. Cocaine and crack are not socially acceptable in all settings/schools. Surveys should be used to determine the acceptability of this drug among your students.

Heroin.   Heroin is a depressant that has many effects similar to alcohol. This drug may be smoked, eaten, or injected. Violence may accompany attempts to get the drug or lower inhibitions to enable one with an aggressive predisposition to behave violently. Heroin is not socially acceptable in all settings/schools. Surveys should be used to determine the acceptability of this drug among your students.

There are certainly other dangerous drugs that students use and abuse, but these are the ones that tend to be most often associated with violence.

Interestingly, at WANTS, on more than one occasion, I heard students mention using marijuana on a regular basis to calm themselves down so they could handle school without becoming violent. As one student put it, "You don't want to see me when I'm not high." I write this to illustrate the complexities of drugs in students' lives and their choices about violence; that is, some students use drugs to self-medicate to *avoid* becoming violent in schools.

Other drugs may be associated with violence in your school. By collecting data using the strategies described earlier in the book, you will be able to examine the ways that students use and abuse drugs and the role of drugs in school violence.

1. Add questions about drug use and abuse to your surveys as you examine the extent of violence and the role of drugs in violence in schools.
2. Identify the drugs that students report using the most and the role these drugs might play in violence in and around the school.
3. Consider components of programs that address students' drug issues.
4. Remember, prevention is the best strategy, and most of the same components for drug prevention are the same for violence prevention. As teachers or administrators, try to focus efforts on

prevention with an eye to addressing intervention issues such as gangs and drugs for referral to appropriate school personnel (e.g., social workers, school psychologists, and counselors) and community agencies (e.g., community mental health and drug treatment facilities).

For more information about different drugs, their role in relationships, violence, and social acceptability issues, see Williams (1998).

Threat Assessment: Determining the Real Danger of Threats

Perhaps the best predictor of serious violence in schools is a student or group of students making a serious threat of violence. In all cases of serious and dangerous violence in schools, students told someone else about their plans. Some plans of deadly violence have been derailed because students have been encouraged to tell adults about the threat. Creating a culture where young people in schools feel safe and comfortable telling adults about the threats their peers make can be one of the most important violence prevention strategies your school adopts. The code of silence that often exists in schools where students do not feel comfortable sharing difficult issues with adults needs to be acknowledged, addressed, and changed to a culture where students feel safe and their confidentiality protected if they report a secret threat that may betray their friends or classmates and risk retaliation.

The U.S. Federal Bureau of Investigation (www.fbi.org) in coordination with Secret Service Agencies has identified a strategy for schools to use called "threat assessment." This strategy involves a step-by-step approach for school personnel to respond to threats of violence. In the wake of serious and lethal violence in schools, personnel have become very sensitive and even overreactive to threats of violence. This program helps determine how dangerous a threat is. Teachers and administrators are trained to critically examine specific threats. Dewey Cornell has created a training program for teachers and administrators that helps them appropriately respond to and analyze threats—threat assessments (Cornell 2002).

For more information about threat assessment techniques espoused by the Secret Service, go to their report online at www.secretservice.gov/ntac_ssi.shtml.

ACTIVITY AND DISCUSSION

Plan a time to get together with your colleagues to discuss ways to infuse anger management, social skills, conflict resolution, and other strategies into your curriculum. Where do these topics seem to logically fit? Do you need more information (e.g., more resources, references, or a training/workshop) to help you with this endeavor?

Think about the ways you can improve your classroom discipline. How can you include students in the process? How can you develop ways to be consistent with the U.S. Constitution, as Forrest Gathercoal argues in *Judicious Discipline*? How can you create consistent, schoolwide discipline plans that are enforced consistently and fairly?

In what ways can you include parents in your plans? Consider ways in which parents will be included and resources you will need to accomplish this.

Discuss with your colleagues other issues such as gangs and drug abuse. Are these problems in the school? How can we find out the extent of the problems? How can we work with community agencies to address these problems?

In what ways do you deal with threats and how do you assess their risk potential? Do you consider all threats equally threatening? Do you have a review process for determining the nature of threats and addressing these risks? Should your school consider reviewing the strategies involved in threat assessment?

4

STEP 4 OF THE PEACE
APPROACH: CHOOSE AND IMPLEMENT

CHOOSE PROGRAMS OR COMPONENTS THAT
FIT THE NEEDS

Now that you have your own personal definition of violence, have a better understanding of your students' issues related to violence in school, and have learned about promising practices that you could implement, the fourth step is to choose a program or program elements that are feasible given limited resources—time and money. The cases used in this book provide examples of choosing and implementing two different strategies that met the needs of students.

To choose a program:

1. Examine the data: What are students' needs?
2. Prioritize needs based on the danger or potential harm for students, feasibility, time, and money.
3. Choose program components to implement that best meet those needs based on program models with demonstrated success.
4. Implement; start small and choose strategies that are possible. Fidelity is essential to successful programs. As you implement programs or components of programs, be sure to follow the directions

for implementation as accurately and carefully as possible. If you are purposefully choosing to modify a program, be sure to specify the ways you are choosing to modify it and why.

At Deerfield, there was an identified need to reduce put-downs. This seemed to be the biggest problem for students, teachers, and administrators—mean treatment (through verbal abuse) and ostracism. They chose the "No Putdowns" program. "No Putdowns" is a comprehensive schoolwide prevention curriculum that has been working with elementary school children in grades K–6 to reduce violence since 1991. Teachers or administrators are trained to administer the program as an integrated part of their existing curriculum or in addition to their existing curriculum. Teachers are given lesson plans, strategies for teaching skills to students, and training to use the materials. The program teaches students a variety of skills (awareness of put-downs, strategies for staying calm in stressful situations, ways to build confidence and self-worth, celebration of diversity, responses to stressful situations and how to choose the best one, ways to build others' self-worth, ways to demonstrate respect, and ways to encourage others). The use of the schoolwide curriculum establishes an environment with a common language for teacher, staff, parent, and child interactions. There is a parental component.

For Deerfield decision makers, the decision to implement "No Putdowns" seemed straightforward. It was relatively inexpensive and it could be infused into the traditional curricular areas. It seemed to address the main needs that teachers, students, and administrators identified.

At WANTS, the needs were greater and the decisions more challenging. There were so many needs and so few resources. The needs were prioritized. Among the top priorities was to find a safe place where students were not crossing gang boundaries. The school was moved to another location where students were not crossing into rival gang territory. There were more security personnel hired for the school. There was a need to help students manage their anger so that they were not so quick to fight when they were angry. Thus, they chose components of various programs based on the anger management competencies outlined in an earlier part of this book. These competencies were created out of a textual analysis of successful programs. There was a need to include caregivers and parents. There was a need to help students transition back to their home schools.

There was a need to have consistent and fairly enforced discipline standards. The components were selected based on the needs of the students at WANTS. The parental component and discipline strategies were discussed in the previous chapter and although these were a part of the strategies at WANTS, they will not be covered again here.

LEARNING BY CASE EXAMPLE: WANTS

As director of the Violence Prevention Project at the local university, I officially formed a partnership with WANTS with the stated purpose of using our grant money to help them address the needs I had identified in my needs assessment. My goal with Catelyn Willey, the new principal (who came in the summer of 1998 with almost no warning because of budget cutbacks and administrative seniority) was to develop a comprehensive approach to violence prevention at the school based on the formal and informal data collected during the previous year. In the summer of 1998, we started to put the following plan in place. The pieces of the "Schoolwide Approach" (see the end of this chapter for complete checklist of items to consider when developing a schoolwide approach) to violence prevention that we used grant money for during the first year were:

- Direct conflict resolution and anger management training to all students;
- Rethinking and developing a new community service component for students;
- In-service training with teachers and curriculum development to infuse anger management and conflict resolution into their existing curricula;
- Parent outreach.

During that year, we also made plans to develop a comprehensive transition program for students returning to their regular schools, and strategies for working more closely with parents.

Before the start of the second year of my work at WANTS, I had to hire a full-time trainer to teach anger management, prosocial skills, problem solving, communication, and conflict resolution skills to students.

I hired an experienced, popular, well-known trainer who was to teach anger management strategies every day (each student once per week for two hours in a group setting).

As of January 25, 1999, there were eighty-seven students on the roster and twelve teachers (four full time), two full-time administrators, a school counselor, a part-time school psychologist, two hall monitors, a school nurse, a full-time secretary, and a police officer. This was nearly double the staff (it was double the number of full-time teaching staff) that had been at the school the previous year.

Also, the school was moved to the newly renovated and historically restored library in the business part of the city. The school moved at the start of the academic year (the start of its fifth year of existence) from the dilapidated former church school building. The building had become available when the funding for the enrichment program that had been in the building was cut just before the start of the school year. The administration needed to fill the space with a program that would be able to move with virtually no notice; WANTS seemed the easiest and smallest program to move. There was much noise made by school board members and other vocal people within the district administration when the nicest building was being given to the "delinquents" at the same time "elementary schools had rats and cockroaches and needed repair." Nonetheless, the school was moved, perhaps mostly because of ease, but it proved to be critical to improving the morale of staff and students. Suddenly, they felt that if they were worthy of such a beautiful space, they must be more important than they had thought. The physical environment of a school can make a huge difference in students' perceptions of themselves and their school.

As mentioned earlier, there were many needs that had been identified during the yearlong examination using interviews, focus groups, observations, and surveys. For example, prior to the start of the 1998–1999 academic year, WANTS had no consistent strategy to teach all students and staff skills such as anger management, conflict resolution, communication, and problem-solving skills (alternatives to violence). We focused our efforts on providing classes in anger management and conflict resolution for all students in the school. We also provided in-service and curriculum development work on these same topics with all of the teachers. In addition, we developed a parent outreach component. Prior to our partnership with WANTS, there was no strategy to involve parents in the school. We hired a part-time social worker to do parent outreach. We worked to create a parent advisory group and are in the process of creating a system of regular communication with parents.

The transition component of the intervention—when students were returned to their original schools—was being developed. We were in the process of examining the fourteen other schools in the district and what their strategies were for transition when some WANTS students were sent back. An additional "transition counselor" was hired to assist students with their transition back to their regular schools and to do family outreach. The transition schools were asked to help develop strategies to facilitate the transition process. The relationships formed during the first year would help us implement this strategy. However, our focus would be on our WANTS partnership and WANTS students.

The Need to Prioritize Solutions

Although we wanted to be able to contribute more at WANTS, based on the needs we identified and the reality of limited resources (time, space, money, and personnel), we focused our contributions to the school as:

- Direct teaching of communication skills, anger management, conflict resolution, and problem solving.
- Integration of anger management, conflict resolution, and prosocial behavior skills training for students in the general curriculum through in-service work with staff.
- Parent outreach and involvement.
- Facilitation of the transition back to regular school for students and their families.

As you embark on an endeavor to choose and implement programs for your school, you will be forced to determine your limitations in terms of resources and to prioritize. Do not let yourself be too frustrated by issues of resources, however. There are local, state, and federal grants available (some on the websites listed in the reference section later in the book), particularly for schools to implement programs with demonstrated success. Having the data to demonstrate a need (as you have already collected in your formal or informal strategies) will also help make a case for grant funding agencies. A word of warning about external funds: when these funds dry up, oftentimes (as was the case at WANTS) so does outside assistance. Try to design and implement programs in house as much as possible so that additional funding is not always critical for successful implementation.

Student Anger Management Training

All students at WANTS were required to attend one two-hour class per week on anger management, conflict resolution, problem solving, communication skills, and skillstreaming (a prosocial skills program with demonstrated success in working with at-risk youth developed by Dr. Arnold Goldstein; see reference in appendix). The course ran the entire academic year and was taught twice daily at WANTS to small groups (fewer than ten students).

The course started in September 1998. Students entered WANTS on a rolling basis, so some students had been in the class since the beginning of the school year and were still in the class. Some of the students who attended the class at the beginning returned to their regular schools. Other students started at some point later in the academic year (October, November, December, or January) and remained in the class through the end of the year. Most students were assigned to WANTS for one calendar year, but some students are assigned for one marking period. The length of time of student participation in the intervention program varied according to the length of time they were assigned to WANTS (based on their superintendent's hearing) and the regularity of their attendance. Although we identified this rolling admission and departure as problematic for teachers and students, this was not viewed as something that could be changed.

The results of a midterm qualitative assessment and the formative evaluation were used to improve our interventions. For example, the anger management course needed to be more individualized—identifying student needs when they entered the class and setting goals for skills they felt they needed to obtain.

Community Service and Carryover of Skills

On the other four days when students were not in anger management class, students were supposed to go to their community service placement site. Annie, whom I hired to teach the class, also coordinated the community service placements for students, following up with students and agencies. This task became burdensome, and students still were not attending their placements regularly. Students liked the idea of doing projects, but they wanted projects that provided some pay. The high school students wanted paid work experience. We worked with students who were old enough to work for pay to help them find paid work experiences when possible.

During the winter of my second year, Annie and I worked with the new principal to reconceptualize the community service component. Consistent with what some of the teachers mentioned in their interviews, we created projects for students that we could link to their academic subject areas. Students were assigned roles in these ten-week projects. Annie and a graduate assistant helped organize the paperwork and oversee the projects. We solicited volunteers from the university and the community to help.

During the fall of 1998 and spring of 1999, we piloted the first of several planned innovative community service projects for students at WANTS based upon student interest. The school principal, Annie, and I developed lists of possible projects, such as a community newsletter, art projects, community gardens, HIV/AIDS education, and day care. The school sought additional funding for these projects. These service projects provided an opportunity to observe students interacting with others to determine if they transferred the skills they learned in the course (anger management, conflict resolution, etc.) to other settings. It was also an opportunity to reinforce the prosocial skills they learned in the class.

We noticed a great deal of change among the students in the pilot projects. One of the most successful projects was an art class where students learned to take others' perspectives and draw pieces of what they could see. Annie would coach students to use the skills in these environments and help students make connections to what they learned in the anger management course. Students loved the hands-on nature of the art class; attendance was very high and students were very motivated. Annie trained some of the supervisors to recognize when students used the skills. Students were praised when they used the skills successfully—or even when they tried. The support of staff was essential to students practicing the anger management and conflict resolution skills outside of class.

WANTS Staff Training

Annie and I conducted training for teachers at WANTS during the summer of 1998. Returning teachers from the 1997–1998 academic year were paid to participate in a three-day workshop where teachers learned anger management skills, judicious discipline, conflict resolution, communication, and problem-solving skills (a reference list of sources is provided in the back of this book). They were also taught how to infuse these skills into their existing subject areas (math, English, social studies, science, business).

Curriculum infusion is a challenging task. Teachers were expected to write lesson plans infusing some of these components into their existing lesson plans. Jerry, the social studies teacher, was the first to complete the assignment, but then he quit WANTS. Paul completed the assignment after working with the university staff. He struggled with the task, as had Jerry, but ultimately completed it. Ken, the business teacher, handed me six lesson plans that he already used, with no attempt to infuse the components. When I talked with him about this, he said, "Kim, it's like I've invited you into my house and now you're trying to move in and take over." He ended up not revising the lesson plans. The other teachers never handed me any drafts of lesson plans.

Teachers still tended to see this idea as a burden, or an add-on, that was detracting from what they were told they had to cover with students. I tried to explain how collaborative learning activities could be used to teach what they were already teaching, and that within collaborative learning groups, students could be taught anger management and conflict resolution. However, some teachers at WANTS were uncomfortable with alternative pedagogy. Discussion and lecture were the popular styles. The veteran teachers had created packets for students to work on independently. In these settings, teachers served the role of tutor. These veteran teachers had developed strategies that they felt worked with this population of students and were reluctant to try the new techniques and subjects described in the workshop.

During the academic year, Annie and I conducted workshops with the entire staff: the administration, counselor, nurse, teaching assistants, teachers, hall monitors, and the police officer. We described the principles of anger management and conflict resolution, and encouraged teachers to build these principles into their teaching, and encouraged others who dealt with students to use the principles. The staff was very supportive and enthusiastic, with the notable exception of some veteran teachers, who often came late to these meetings and talked amongst themselves during small-group sessions. This form of resistance suggested to me that the veteran teachers felt they had found strategies that worked for them and did not want to learn others. Raji told me one day that the reason she did not look for jobs in the regular school is that she had already developed her packets for the WANTS students and would need to start again and do more work if she moved to a "regular" school.

Attendance

Attendance rates at alternative education sites for at-risk youth have historically been low. At WANTS, the average daily rate of attendance was 60 percent during both years of my observations. Students were savvy and knew ways around the system, so they could avoid attending WANTS. Students who were sixteen years old or older did not have to attend school of any kind and many did drop out. The students who were under sixteen would attend somewhat more regularly, but many were placed on probation for truancy—although it was rare that any kind of penalty would result.

Any program addressing the needs of the students most at risk of violence and aggression needs to address the issue of attendance. Working with community agencies conducting street outreach and those who hire street outreach workers is a start. Also, most schools have truancy officers. It is important to work closely with these individuals. In addition, the parent outreach should involve regular feedback about attendance. Parents need to be aware of their child's lack of attendance and a partnership needs to be formed to get students to school on a regular basis. Also, there must to be structures in place that work closely with regularly absent students once they have been identified—a system of calling or even picking up students in the morning. These students are perhaps the most at risk of criminal behavior when they are not in school.

Aftercare and Transition

An examination of the comprehensive bibliography compiled by the Hamilton Fish National Institute (available at http://hamfish.org/pub/altedbib.html) about alternative education for violent youth shows that the aspect of alternative education most consistently neglected is the student's transition back to his or her home school. At WANTS we found this to be the case as well. The transition back was largely ignored and many students would ultimately drop out of school shortly upon their re-entry to their home schools. As a result, we hired a graduate assistant to work with WANTS students during the year when they returned to their regular schools to help students with the challenging transition back.

In the fall of 1999, WANTS teachers and others worked with students through their first year of transition on academic and social issues. Teachers provided academic support and made referrals to additional support as needed. They worked closely with the social worker to make appropriate referrals for the student and his or her family.

Issues of transition must be addressed for any student who is taken out of the mainstream classroom. This should include *any* time out of the classroom for poor behavior (suspension, expulsion, or even in-school suspension), time out for incarceration, or other mental health treatment. Any time a child is out of the classroom, plans need to be in place to help him or her re-enter.

Pedagogy Using Media and Collaboration

Teachers are often reluctant to use videos and other forms of media in their classrooms. However, when done well and used to reinforce good teaching, these media forms—particularly videos—are very effective ways to capture the attention of challenging students. We need to develop better tools for students that capitalize on our myriad of media forms (computers, televisions, video, and so on). We need to acknowledge that students respond well to various forms of media and provide opportunities for students to interact with media forms as often as possible. Unfortunately, in poorer, urban districts where these forms of media are perhaps even more necessary, the equipment is unavailable. This requires teachers and administrators to be creative. Partnerships with local colleges or universities for undergraduate volunteers to work with youth on campus with different media forms and collaboration with local agencies for funding for supplies are two possible strategies. I do not mean to suggest that use of media be used to supplant the work that teachers need to do to teach basic skills of literacy and math and the other subject areas, but that these alternative forms of media be used to support more traditional strategies.

In addition to media, more collaborative forms of pedagogy need to be employed in the classroom. Developing a culture of cooperation rather than competition results in students learning how to create win-win situations instead of win-lose situations. Cooperative learning strategies have been shown to create less violent and less aggressive classrooms. Students learn to value other students as colleagues rather than competitors. This culture of cooperation creates the foundation for developing a caring school.

Creating a Caring Environment

Within the schoolwide approach model, there needs to be a strategic way to teach care and how to build caring relationships. Nel Noddings's book, *A Challenge to Care in Schools*, described the importance of teaching students how to care and how to be cared for. She also describes the importance of creating a caring school environment. She wrote (1992, 16), "My description of a caring relation does not entail that carer and cared-for are permanent labels for individuals. Mature relationships are characterized by mutuality. They are made up of strings of encounters in which the parties exchange places; both members are carers and cared-fors as opportunities arise." There were some examples of students demonstrating caring for each other and for teachers, and there were some examples of staff caring for students and other staff. Caring needs to become a central component of any school environment—especially for students who are identified as being at risk for violent behavior.

Considering Prenatal and Postnatal Care as Violence Prevention Strategies

It may seem strange to read about the importance of prenatal and postnatal care in developing a whole-school approach to violence prevention; however, I believe we need to incorporate these notions into our thinking. A truly comprehensive approach to violence prevention needs to address the needs of young people from the earliest possible point. As I noticed at WANTS, there were pregnant and parenting teens with no guidance whatsoever about how to care for themselves during pregnancy or how to take care of an infant. I heard many stories of pregnant teens using drugs (particularly alcohol and marijuana) without thought to the impact on the fetus. I heard stories from social workers working with these young people after their infants were born who were abusive or at least overly rough with their newborns, and who admitted that they did not know how to hold or care for their babies. These babies are at risk of growing up and being aggressive or violent in school. More work needs to be done to examine the links between the lack of parental attachment and violence. Also, we need to better understand the connection between maternal drug use and resulting aggression in the offspring later in life. In the meantime, schools can be poised to be proactive by working with pregnant and parenting teens to be drug-free, positive, caring role models for their children. Providing skills for parents to read to their children and spend quality caring time together is one way, but there are many. This is perhaps the earliest proactive strategy to reduce violence that schools can use. Schools cannot ignore this charge. The long-term effects will likely be very dramatic.

LEARNING BY CASE EXAMPLE: DEERFIELD

Unlike WANTS, which had complex and multiple needs and needed correspondingly complex solutions, Deerfield's problems seemed more straightforward. They, like many schools, decided to purchase an existing, developed program. The "No Putdowns" program seemed to meet their needs. Choosing existing programs from the many programs that have had demonstrated success can be easier than constructing programs tailored to meet the specific needs of your school, but may not meet all the needs or may have components or program elements that are not appropriate.

ACTIVITY AND DISCUSSION

Choosing programs or components of programs is challenging. There are many programs and components to choose from. Different people have heard different things about various programs and have preformed bias for or against programs. Try to keep the identified, prioritized needs in mind (based on the formal and informal data you collected) and the programs best equipped to address these needs (that you determined from the chapter on advocating for the needs of students). You need to consider:

- Your priorities (based on your data)
- Your limitations (funding, personnel, time)
- Possible strategies to gain more resources (grant writing, fund raisers, etc.)

Then, with your colleagues, choose a program or program elements that seem to best suit the needs your students expressed to you and are possible given your limitations. Consider the examples from the case studies: "No Putdowns" versus anger management examples and whole-school approaches versus more targeted interventions.

Preferably, try to have the interventions you select be those that other teachers or administrators will use as well. A whole-school approach is ideal. Implement the strategies or components into your classroom, which could include:

- Curriculum infusion or training of anger management and conflict resolution competencies
- Discipline planning
- Parental involvement

The following is a checklist of issues to consider when trying to choose and implement a schoolwide approach collaboratively with other teachers and administrators:

—— 1. Identification and programming for students most at risk of violence (intensive case management, social skills training, etc.)

—— 2. Addressing multicultural education needs in curricula and in school activities

—— 3. Development of programs that teach caring and help create a caring school environment where caring is modeled and rewarded

—— 4. Creation of a discipline program that is consistent, fair, and that all students and staff understand

—— 5. Pedagogy that is cooperative and collaborative instead of competitive and that incorporates ways that students learn best

—— 6. Opportunities to teach conflict resolution, anger management, and problem solving to all staff and students (directly and using curriculum infusion)

—— 7. Peer mediation as a prevention strategy (including peer-peer, parent-child, teacher-student, gangs, and other members of the community in mediation practices)

—— 8. Parental involvement encouraged (including outreach, home visits, regular communication between teachers and parents)

—— 9. Community involvement (including tutoring and mentoring programs, GED programs)

—— 10. Alternative education sites for some students

—— 11. Transition programs for all students new to a building, including those from alternative education sites as well as any time a student is removed and returned from class

—— 12. Environmental issues addressed:
    —— One entry and exit with greeter
    —— Security in hot spots, including teachers or administrators
    —— Prevention of weapon concealment in clothes and packs

—— No graffiti

—— Clean and welcoming building

—— 13. Drug education and treatment (or appropriate referrals) for students and parents

—— 14. Collaboration with all major stakeholders in a child's life

—— 15. Activities, including academic enrichment, during after-school hours

—— 16. Plans to identify and address academic needs, especially poor literacy among students and their families

—— 17. Prenatal care and postnatal care for at-risk parenting teens

—— 18. Comprehensive evaluation plan in place

    —— Qualitative components (interviews, observations, and focus groups)

    —— Quantitative components (pretest, posttest, comparison groups)

5

STEP 5 OF THE PEACE
APPROACH: EVALUATE

Often omitted, but incredibly important in violence prevention is evaluation. Evaluation takes time and resources that are often in short supply. Evaluation needs to be viewed as an essential component of our programs. We need to assess what is working in our schools and what is not. This should not be used as an excuse to throw things out and start anew every year, but rather to refine and improve strategies and components.

THE FORGOTTEN ART OF EVALUATION

Too often, we begin projects based on intuition rather than evidence, and we try something else before we have an opportunity to assess whether what we tried in the first place was "successful." Determining the "success" or "failure" of a program is complicated. Consider the following:

1. We need to determine what we mean by success and failure. This is not always the same for all involved. We need to think about and document what "success" would look like versus what "failure" would look like.

2. We need to examine if the objectives we set for a program have been attained. We can do this through a variety of qualitative (similar to our informal approaches discussed in chapter 2) and quantitative (similar to our formal approaches discussed in chapter 2) approaches.
3. We need to continue to refine and adjust program components based on new evidence from all stakeholders.

Qualitative approaches to evaluation:

- Interviews
- Focus groups
- Observations
- Journal writing
- Teacher-made surveys (open-ended or Likert-type questions)

Quantitative approaches:

- Experimental design (using pretest/posttest comparison with comparison/control group)
- Statistical analyses of significant differences before and after implementation

Determining "Success" or "Failure"

1. Identify objectives of the program: What did you hope to accomplish? (Base this on data collected from stakeholders.)
2. How can you best and most realistically measure whether you met the stated objectives of your prevention/intervention strategies? This can include qualitative, quantitative, or a combination of strategies.
3. Put your plan in place. Be sure to have personnel, time, and support to accomplish this.

Different stakeholders and participants in a school community have various definitions of what successful violence prevention or intervention programs need to achieve. Objectives should be set that are measurable, reasonable, and attainable. The objectives must be based on what those most intimately involved (students and school personnel) with the school consistently claim that they need. Objectives may be identified through interviews, observations, surveys, or focus groups with students and staff. However these data are collected, students and staff must have a voice and perceive that they had input in the development of the objectives.

Preparation of objectives brings us back to an earlier point about our own personal definitions of violence as well as others' views, and what gets considered and what gets left out. Objectives need to consider less obvious forms of violence (sexual harassment, bullying, verbal assaults, etc.) as well as the more obvious forms of physical violence (hitting, punching, fighting, weapon carrying, etc.). In addition, we need to examine whether students are meeting their personal goals: Are they getting into colleges, graduating from high school, getting jobs? Or are many students ending up incarcerated or on probation (as was the case at WANTS)?

Once each school or setting defines its objectives for "success," we need to create ways to measure if a program has been successful. This can be best accomplished through a combination of formal and informal methods—mostly the same ones identified in the second step of the PEACE plan. If one wants to examine *how* an intervention has worked and how individuals *made sense* of the intervention, informal measures such as interviewing, focus groups, journal writing, and observations will yield this information. If one wants to determine *if* an intervention or particular components of an intervention worked, experimental designs using already created surveys (also described in chapter 2) may prove useful. Plus, if you used a formal or informal survey to collect data about student needs, you will already have "pretest" or "baseline" data from which to demonstrate improvement that you can attribute to your program.

Evaluation is always challenging, and frequently those involved in overseeing a new intervention neglect to obtain baseline or initial data about the school prior to the intervention to determine any changes for the better. Before embarking on development of a schoolwide project such as the one described in this chapter, collecting data you might already have will help:

- Baseline data through surveys done before starting the program
- Archival data including:
  ◦ suspension reports
  ◦ office records (behavior referrals, attendance rates, test scores, etc.)
  ◦ police data for the area around the school
- Focus groups and interviews with staff, parents, and students
- Observations of trouble spots in the school

Some of these are the same methods described in chapter 2, but now we employ them after the intervention has been in place for a year to determine if there has been any change. We need to understand how individuals within a given setting have been changed for the better (if at all) by a given intervention. Do they *feel* safer? Are they *actually* safer? Are those in the culture less likely to act aggressively?

Frequently, school officials are afraid to collect data that may show their intervention has been unsuccessful. Understandably, they feel this lack of success will reflect poorly on them. However, evaluation should be viewed as a way to better understand and improve a given intervention. Well-designed evaluations allow us to examine the effectiveness of different components to see what might be working. The key to a successful intervention is effective evaluation, which uses a variety of measures to determine what seems to be working most effectively to reduce violence in schools.

As teachers or administrators, you can design your own informal or formal strategies for demonstrating what is working. The following examples from the case studies demonstrate the difference in the kinds of data you can collect when conducting evaluations of your programs and how you can use them. Mostly, these represent formal approaches to evaluation, but there are informal components within these examples you can implement as well.

EVALUATION AT DEERFIELD

At Deerfield, I conducted a formal and informal analysis of the "No Put-downs" program to determine its effectiveness. Not all schools will have the time or luxury of conducting both formal and informal evaluations of their programs, but ideally these strategies when used together give us a good picture of what works and what does not.

Choosing a Comparison School or Group

One of the best ways to determine if a program works is to compare it before and after it is implemented to another similar group of students who did not have the program (a comparison group). Deerfield Middle

School implemented the "No Putdowns" program during the fall of 1999. To serve as a comparison school, a neighboring school of similar size, socioeconomic class, and racial makeup, Tug Hill School, was selected. I created the surveys from the objectives of the program and from questions that I had as a result of observations, focus groups, and interviews. Pretests were given before the start of the "No Putdowns" program and the posttests were given at the end of the school year to both schools.

Informal Results

The results from observations, interviews, and focus groups at Deerfield indicated that students felt positive about the program and could see benefits from the program (students were nicer to one another and there were fewer fights). Students acknowledged that they were more aware of their own use and others' use of put-downs. However, students also said that the more "popular students," albeit nicer in general, came up with new and creative put-downs that teachers or administrators did not know. The creative use of put-downs was an integral part of popularity, particularly for boys.

Teachers at Deerfield had mixed feelings about the program. Some teachers did not feel equipped to do the lessons (citing lack of time, unfamiliarity with the material, poor student response, and feeling the program was not necessary or effective). Some teachers were positive, reporting that they liked the fact that the program gave them a "common language to use with students" and that it gave some concrete ways for students to deal with conflicts without fighting. Veteran teachers tended to be the most skeptical, reporting that "we do this anyway." Ironically, a couple of powerful veteran teachers at one school (which was initially in the study but later dropped) bullied less experienced teachers into rallying the teachers' union to support them to not implement the program and evaluation. Some teachers liked the program, reporting that they liked the skills that students learned and a common language and strategy.

Administrators generally felt that there were fewer office referrals, that teachers were handling conflicts in the classroom more often, and students were less cruel to each other. Nevertheless, administrators acknowledged that some teachers complained about the program (particularly veteran teachers) and did not see a reason to have it. Administrators agreed that continuing to motivate teachers to use the lessons and reinforce the skills was one of the most challenging tasks to program success.

Survey Results

Because the survey questions required "yes" or "no" answers, statistical analyses using these kinds of variables were used to compare pretest and posttest results as well as comparisons with the comparison school. Statistical analysis is not always necessary, but if schools want to examine statistically significant results, then it becomes an important task. It is possible to examine survey results for percentage changes in students' experiences and perspectives, as is the case in the survey shown in table 2.2.

Deerfield Pretest and Posttest Comparison

Deerfield sixth grade was used to examine if a single grade within a school could successfully implement the "No Putdowns" program with positive results. Only the sixth grade of Deerfield Middle School (grades 5–7) implemented the "No Putdowns" program. Comparing Deerfield sixth-grade student survey results prior to the implementation of the "No Putdowns" program (administered in October 1999 to 128 students) to the student survey completed at the conclusion of the first year of the "No Putdowns" program (administered in May 2000 to 148 students), the following statistically significant differences were found:

There were significant *increases* in the number of students who reported "yes" on the following questions at posttest:

1. Students in this school sometimes use put-downs
2. Students say mean things a lot in school
3. Do you sometimes put others down or say mean things to others in school?
4. Have others picked on you on the bus in the past two months?
5. Do some people think you're mean in school or on the bus?

At first glance, one might conclude the program actually caused more problems than it solved. However, focus groups and observations revealed that these increases were most likely an indication that students had become more aware of their own use and others' use of put-downs and mean behavior. They also became more aware of others' perceptions of themselves. These were goals of the program.

There were significant *decreases* in the number of students who reported "yes" to the following questions at posttest:

1. Put-downs hurt my feelings.
2. Do you feel safe in school?
3. Do you like school?
4. Do you like most of your classes?
5. Have you hit anyone at school or on the bus in the past two months?
6. Have you been hit in school or on the bus in the past two months?

Deerfield Compared to Comparison Group

At pretest, there were no significant differences between the comparison group (Tug Hill sixth-grade cohort, which did not have the "No Putdowns" program) and the experimental group (Deerfield sixth grade, which did have the "No Putdowns" program), except on the measure of students being "picked on" in school or on the bus where the numbers were significantly higher among the control group at pretest. The other measures were not significantly different.

The most fundamental goal of the "No Putdowns" program was changing student behavior, so the analysis here focused on the questions that dealt with school violence behaviors (victimization, ostracism, and perpetration). The posttest groups were compared, and the differences were not as dramatic without comparing the comparison group to the "No Putdowns" sites by grade level, indicating that the most significant changes in behavior happened at the higher grade levels, specifically the sixth grade. When comparing the sixth-grade population at Deerfield with the sixth-grade population at Tug Hill, there were significant differences between the two groups on the following variables at posttest, although there had been no significant differences at pretest:

1. Students who said that they had been picked on in school or on the bus in the past two months (victimization) (Tug Hill = 65 percent versus Deerfield at 38 percent)

2. Students who said they had been in a fight in school in the past two months (violent behavior) (Tug Hill = 40 percent, Deerfield = 18 percent)
3. Students who felt left out when groups played on the playground (ostracism) (Tug Hill = 48 percent, Deerfield = 32 percent)
4. Students who agreed that they had hit someone in the past two months (perpetration) (Tug Hill = 29 percent, Deerfield = 13 percent)
5. Students who agreed that they have been hit in school or on the bus in the past two months (victimization) (Tug Hill = 50 percent, Deerfield = 27 percent)

Even without sophisticated statistical analyses, we can see here the dramatic differences between the two groups after the first year of the intervention at Deerfield. Comparing percentages can be a powerful tool for schools that may not be able to conduct more sophisticated statistics.

Summary of Results

Increased awareness of put-downs by self and others. There was a significant increase in awareness of put-downs and cruel behavior, including one's own behavior and that of others, that resulted in dramatic increases in the measures that asked students about their own and others' use put-downs, saying mean things. Students felt that put-downs did not hurt their feelings as much at the time of the posttest as they did during the pretest. The qualitative results supported these notions as nearly all students in interviews and focus groups said that they were more aware of their own use and others' use of put-downs and mean behavior as a result of the program.

Decreased satisfaction and sense of safety. Deerfield sixth-grade students felt significantly less safe in school, and liked their classes and school significantly less than they did in the beginning of the year. Unfortunately, no posttest data were collected at the comparison school to determine if these feelings were a maturational function of the age and grade level, but it is interesting to note that students felt less safe and happy in school at the end of the year after the "No Putdowns" program. This association needs to be addressed by school personnel who may wrongly assume that because schools *are* safer, that students *feel* safer.

The good news: Actual change in violent behaviors. What was significantly reduced at Deerfield were actual violent behaviors—experiences as both perpetrator and victim (hitting, being hit, fighting) had significantly declined by the posttest. These behaviors showed a significant reduction when compared to the sixth-grade cohort in the comparison school and when compared to the pretest data at the experimental school site.

In conclusion, at Deerfield in the sixth grade, an increased awareness of put-downs and mean behavior resulted in increased reports of put-downs and mean behavior of self and others. Perhaps this increased awareness in problem behaviors was the cause of decreased perceptions of safety and satisfaction with school. Despite these perceptions, actual behavior related to violence was significantly decreased when compared to the sixth-grade cohort in the comparison school.

Conclusions from Data

The data demonstrated at Deerfield Middle School that there were significantly more reports of put-downs (likely due to increased awareness) and a reduction in perceptions of feeling safe in school and on the bus (again, likely due to increased awareness of put-downs). Despite these increases, there were significant reductions in violent behavior such as fighting, hitting, and being hit when compared to the pretest and to the cohorts in the comparison school.

The data indicated some dramatic gender differences among the topics that "No Putdowns" addresses for youth. Boys were more likely to report the use of put-downs and being mean to others. Boys were more likely to be both victims and perpetrators of physical violence (hitting and fighting) and more likely to feel unsafe in school and on the bus and to be less satisfied in school. Girls were slightly more likely to experience ostracism and to be more aware of others' use of put-downs. Girls were also more likely to indicate that put-downs hurt their feelings. There were no gender differences for fighting. Also, previous research indicates that girls experience many types of harassment—particularly various forms of sexual harassment—that "No Putdowns" does not specifically address, nor did the evaluation. More work needs to be done to determine the impact of this program, specifically on sexual harassment and other issues for girls.

Recommendations and Implications Based on the Data

As a teacher, having evidence to support the success of your program is essential to keeping it going, getting more support, and sometimes getting much-needed recognition. Data can also help you make some recommendations of additional needs. The sixth grade at Deerfield Middle School was used to examine the impact of a schoolwide intervention if a single grade implemented it without the rest of the school. The sixth-grade results demonstrated that the program had an impact without being a schoolwide intervention. Clearly, the qualitative data demonstrate that children felt that the sites where others had not been through the program (the bus, the cafeteria, and the hallways when they intersected with other grades that had not had "No Putdowns") were areas where put-downs and problem behavior needed to be addressed. Ideally, the program should be implemented as a schoolwide or districtwide intervention, but the results indicate that this is not essential. Although it is not advisable, it seems to be supported that you can be successful as an island if you should choose to implement these strategies without support.

The "No Putdowns" program at Deerfield demonstrated success at reducing some of the most problematic behaviors in schools today (hitting and fighting), particularly among the students for whom these behaviors are the most challenging (the sixth grade). Despite a reduction in problematic behaviors such as hitting and fighting, students felt less safe. The qualitative data suggest that these reports are likely because of an increased awareness in one's own use and others' use of put-downs, although likely responsible for a decrease in violent behaviors, and may be responsible for students' feeling less safe in school and on the bus. Awareness of any problem often makes those who are most at risk of experiencing the problem more fearful. School violence is only one such problem. More analysis needs to be conducted to unravel some of these questions. Nevertheless, this is helpful information for teachers to know.

These results help us better understand what works in school environments to reduce violent acts such as hitting and fighting. A program can meet its stated objectives and have other issues that need to be addressed. More work needs to be done to determine the long-term impact on schoolwide programs such as "No Putdowns" and the components that have demonstrated success in reducing violent behaviors.

EVALUATING EFFECTIVENESS AT WANTS

At WANTS, there was a formal approach to evaluation. A formal, nationally tested survey was used before the start of the intervention and at the end of the year. These results give us some idea of the kinds of feedback we can get from more formalized surveys.

Pretest and Posttest Results at WANTS

The National School Crime and Safety Survey was administered in September 1998 to students at WANTS. Pretest and posttest surveys were used in conjunction with other informal data collected. In the alternative school, forty-three students in grades 7 through 12 (72 percent of the students were in grades 7 through 9, 35.7 percent were males, and 64.3 percent females) completed the pretest questionnaire. At the conclusion of the formative year (May 1999), forty-one students completed the posttest (eleven of whom had completed the pretest)—73.2 percent in grades 7 through 9, 55 percent male and 45 percent female.

Only 38 percent of students reported that they could keep from getting very angry at the pretest (i.e., they agreed or strongly agreed with the statement "I can keep from getting really angry"). The posttest data revealed that significantly more students (52 percent) could keep from getting very angry, indicating that they thought they had become better able to handle their anger since they came to the school. Also, 60.7 percent of students taking the posttest revealed that they had become better able to deal with conflicts with their friends, acquaintances, and family without becoming violent since they came to the alternative school. This result was significantly higher than those taking the pretest who reported that they could not keep from getting very angry. Approximately 64 percent of students agreed or strongly agreed with the statement that they would get into a fight if someone disrespected them at the time of the pretest, compared with 14.7 percent of students taking the posttest. This demonstrated a significant reduction in the number of students who reported a willingness to fight because they were disrespected.

Among the goals of teaching school staff ways to infuse anger management into their curriculum was to improve students' ability to manage their anger. Students reported an improved ability to recognize their anger cues and triggers and to handle their anger without becoming violent. The second major goal of the program was to reduce the number of everyday student fights that resulted from feeling "disrespected" (a major cause of fights in the school). This number was dramatically reduced. Finally, one major goal of involving the faculty and staff in the anger management curriculum development was to reduce the number of students who felt disrespected by school staff. This was not achieved, as there was not a significant change between those in the pretest group and those in the posttest.

Upon completion of the anger management course and the benefit of courses with anger management infused throughout, students were asked to report on their ability to manage their anger and handle conflict. Eleven of the forty-one respondents had completed the pretest because of high student turnover throughout the year. Nearly half (45.5 percent) had been at the alternative school since January 1999 and participated in the program since then. Most of the students had several months of the interventions before taking the posttest.

At posttest, most of the students (86.2 percent) believed that they were good at listening to others, and 41.4 percent thought they had become better listeners since they came to the alternative school. Most of the students (more than 75 percent) answered positively that they thought they were good communicators (i.e., could recognize their own and others' body language, could get others to listen to them without threatening them). Nevertheless, most of the students reported that when somebody made them angry, they wanted to fight (55.6 percent) even though most students (92.9 percent and 75 percent respectively) reported that they could recognize when they were getting angry and knew what to do to calm themselves when they became angry. Although 51.7 percent reported that they had become better able to handle their anger since they came to the alternative school, only 20.7 percent said they usually walk away from an argument, 39.3 percent said that they usually tried to talk to the person with whom they were in conflict, and 82.8 percent said that they usually would physically fight if they were having a fight or argument. At the conclusion of their time at the alternative school, many students attributed their improved ability to handle conflict and anger to their time at the school where they learned anger management directly and had these skills reinforced in their traditional curricula.

The School Environment and Staff Perspectives

Throughout the school year, assessment was conducted by analyzing field notes collected during observations of and interviews with staff and students for emerging themes. I examined field notes for themes related to students' and teachers' reactions to the programs as well as students' changes in violent and aggressive attitudes and behaviors. Classroom observations and interviews with students and teachers were used to gather data about the daily working of the school and the interventions.

At WANTS, preceding curriculum infusion, teacher training, and comprehensive efforts to reduce violence in the school, student and staff reports of the school were profoundly negative. Interviews, observations at staff meetings and classes, and focus groups yielded much evidence of frustration and dissatisfaction with the school. The year after implementing the intervention strategies, most students reported that they liked the school very much and felt comfortable and secure there. All of the students interviewed felt that the teachers were very helpful and attempted to help them and work with them. However, as one student stated, "[The school] is very easy." Few students felt they had to work very hard. This lack of academic rigor placed them far behind their peers when returning to the regular schools.

Interviews were conducted with staff, students, and parents, and observational data were collected. Compared to the previous year, students all said that they liked the school and felt comfortable and safe. Students were interviewed before their return to their regular schools. Despite liking their experience at the school and feeling like they "learned their lesson," most were excited to return. However, many parents wanted their children to stay as long as possible because the school provided smaller classes and more individualized attention. Most of the parents described their children as having difficulty in school, but that they thought they were doing better academically and socially in the more intimate setting. Teachers noticed a difference, too. They said there was more of a feeling of community in the school than the previous years when teachers would come in, teach their classes, and leave. Teachers would come in early and stay late. They came to activities. The tone at staff meetings was no longer one of hostility and frustration—it had become one of collaboration and fun.

Staff Survey Results

Staff at WANTS completed a posttest created by the Hamilton Fish National Institute with questions about their experiences in the school and their perceptions of the interventions. Sixteen teachers, administrators, and other school staff were given a survey at the conclusion of the first year of the intervention. Most teachers prior to the intervention complained that students rarely treated adults in the school with respect. At the end of the first year, only 13.3 percent of the staff agreed with the statement "Students rarely treat school personnel with respect." All of the staff agreed that school personnel were respectful to students, and all except 13.3 percent felt that students received appropriate punishment for infractions.

Compared to the previous school year when the school was located in one of the more notorious sections of the city, all staff at the end of the intervention year (when the school was located in the heart of the downtown business district) reported feeling moderately to very safe in the building during and after class hours.

Nearly 90 percent of staff reported that they were moderately to highly satisfied with the violence prevention activities (direct anger management and staff training), 93.3 percent felt that violence prevention knowledge improved among student participants, and 73.3 percent felt that violence-related attitudes and beliefs among the student participants improved. Over 93 percent of staff felt that relationships between student participants in the anger management project had improved. All staff members said they would recommend the interventions to other schools.

The overwhelmingly positive staff ratings of the school and the intervention indicate that during the first year of the intervention, there was a dramatic improvement in the overall attitude of staff at the school. Some of this improvement may be attributed to the anger management training of students and staff and the work with teachers on infusion, but there were many changes happening in the school simultaneously. First, the new building was a beautifully restored historical library compared to the previous site that was a dilapidated former Catholic school. Second, there was a change in leadership—the school received a new principal who was a thirty-five-year veteran of the district and had the power to make changes that teachers wanted. Third, the administration supported the programs and thus, the teachers were more involved with the interventions and in supporting them. Fourth, more full-time staff members were added, including more teachers. There had previously been no police officer or security guard. During the year of the intervention, they had hired a full-time police officer and security guard. This made staff and students feel safer. Also, all staff and students mentioned the presence of the anger management trainer who modeled the behavior she taught. She was respectful of students and staff and worked with them to resolve conflicts nonviolently. Her room became a safe haven for students and staff alike—where all were expected to be respectful and kind. Clearly, no intervention exists in a vacuum. There are always other factors at work. However, it is important to recognize how individuals make sense of these factors and their impact on their lives. Students and teachers alike felt better about being at the school.

LESSONS WE CAN LEARN

Evaluation takes time, and time is a commodity that teachers or administrators often do not have. However, it is important to figure out how to make time to evaluate what we do to see if it is working—or what parts of our programs are working. Not all types of evaluation can be used in all cases. Sometimes it may be possible to use mostly informal strategies such as observing students, speaking with students in interviews or focus groups, or creating and administering your own informal surveys. Sometimes you can use formal strategies such as those used at Deerfield (including a comparison school) or WANTS (using a nationally developed survey). Sometimes you can use a combination of formal and informal strategies, as was the case at both WANTS and Deerfield. The goal is finding out what has changed as a result of your intervention. Collecting information before the start (which also gives a picture of the needs of your students) and collecting information after the intervention has been underway for at least a year should yield some constructive feedback. Evaluation should not be used as a punitive device to scrap a program entirely, but should provide helpful, critical feedback that can inform and ultimately improve the practice. Investing in a program that is consistently not yielding *any* successful results is a greater waste of time. It would be useful to know if, year after year, you are not finding positive results. Likewise, it would be helpful to know if a program is im- proving relationships among students and reducing violent behavior, as was found at Deerfield and at WANTS.

Sometimes a good strategy for busy teachers or administrators is to team up with a teacher-educator at a local college or university inter- ested in school issues related to violence or evaluation. Collaboration to help with the sometimes overwhelming task of evaluation is helpful and may prove to be mutually beneficial for the collaborators. Also, most grant-funded violence prevention activities require evaluation and build in money to hire an outside evaluator. Hiring outside evaluators when possible is very helpful for lifting the burden of responsibility of evaluation. Nevertheless, individuals in the school should be involved closely with the evaluator to make sure she or he is using appropriate strategies and providing useful reports and feedback about programs and components.

ACTIVITY AND DISCUSSION

Evaluation is a challenging art. Sometimes schools choose to have out- side agencies evaluate their programs. This is a good approach for schools that can afford it. There are other methods that are feasible for schools to undertake. Consider the following options:

Qualitative or informal strategies:

- Observations (Is violent behavior or problem behavior actually re- duced?)

- Interviews with staff and students (Do staff and students feel safer? Do they experience less violence in school? Do they see fewer of the problematic behaviors identified?)
- Journal assignments (Consider ways that students could keep journals and reflect on the role of violence in their lives.)
- Focus groups with staff and students (What is really happening in school since the intervention has been implemented? Are there noticeable changes for the better? What aspects of the program or components do students like most? Teachers or administrators? What is most problematic to implement?)

Quantitative or formal strategies:

- Pretest/posttest: Pretest using one of the surveys described in the chapters, then compare to posttest results.
- Choose a comparison school or even comparison classroom without the program (as in the Deerfield example) and compare pretest and posttest results.
- Examine numbers (e.g., discipline referrals, expulsions or suspensions for violent infractions).

AFTERWORD

The two vastly different case studies described in this book demonstrate the usefulness of using the PEACE approach as a general framework for making decisions and planning violence prevention and intervention strategies in schools.

Planning violence prevention in schools is time-consuming work, but it is worth investing the time at the front end to create meaningful programs to address the particular needs of each school.

This book provides an outline of an approach and some places to go for more information. Use the references in the back as well as the websites throughout the text.

The PEACE approach (Personalize, Examine experiences of students, Advocate based on needs, Choose and implement, and Evaluate programs) is not as linear as this book may make it seem. Evaluation informs our choices; our personal opinions and experiences shift and change, which affects what we notice among our students, and we may use our evaluation to reexamine our students' perspectives. The strategies are complex. The work is challenging but is essential to the lives and welfare of our children.

GOOD LUCK!!

APPENDIX

A LIST OF REFERENCES

In addition to the references listed in this book, there are a number of useful resources you might find helpful in your planning and with the development of a schoolwide approach to violence prevention.

Achenbach, T. M. 1991. *Teacher's Report Form.* Burlington: University of Vermont Department of Psychiatry.

Apple, M. 1990. The hidden curriculum and the nature of conflict. In *Ideology and Curriculum.* 2d ed. New York: Routledge.

Berman, S., and P. LaFarge, eds. 1993. *Promising practices in teaching social responsibility.* New York: SUNY Press.

Brown, L., and J. Leigh. 1986. *Adaptive Behavior Inventory.* Austin, Tex.: Pro-Ed.

Burstyn, J. N., ed. 1997. *Educating tomorrow's valuable citizen.* Albany: SUNY Press.

Burstyn, J. N., G. Bender, R. Casella, H. W. Gordon, D. P. Guerra, K. V. Luschen, R. Stevens, and K. M. Williams. 2001. *Preventing violence in schools: A challenge to American democracy.* Mahwah, N.J.: Lawrence Erlbaum.

Burstyn, J. N., and R. Stevens. 1998. Education in conflict resolution: A whole-school approach. *Nexus: Journal of Peace, Conflict and Social Change* 1, no. 1.

Canada, G. 1995. *Fist, stick, knife, gun: A personal history of vsiolence in America.* Boston: Beacon Press.

Carlsson-Paige, N., and D. E. Levin. 1987. *Who's calling the shots? How to respond effectively to children's fascination with war play and war toys.* Philadelphia: New Society.

De Bono, E. 1990. *Lateral thinking: Creativity step by step.* New York: Harper and Row.

Delpit, L. 1995. *Other people's children: Cultural conflict in the classroom.* New York: New Press.

Epp, J. R., and A. M. Watkinson. 1996. *Systemic violence: How schools hurt children.* London: Falmer Press.

Galtung, J. 1969. Violence, peace, and peace research. *Journal of Peace Research,* 167–91.

Gathercoal, F. 1997. *Judicious discipline.* San Francisco: Caddo Gap Press.

Goldstein, A., and E. McGinnis. 1997. *Skillstreaming the adolescent: New strategies and perspectives for teaching prosocial skills.* Champaign, Ill.: Research Press.

Goodwillie, S., ed. 1993. *Voices from the future: Our children tell us about violence in America.* New York: Crown.

Grundy, S. 1987. *Curriculum: Product or praxis?* New York: Falmer Press.

Hamburg, D. A. 1994. *Education for conflict resolution.* Report of the President, Carnegie Corporation of New York.

Harris, I. M. 1990. Principles of peace pedagogy. *Peace and Change* 15, no. 3: 254–71.

Hernandez, A. 1998. *Peace in the streets: Breaking the cycle of gang violence.* Washington, D.C.: Child Welfare League of America.

Hoffman, A. M. 1996. *Schools, violence, and society.* Westport, Conn.: Praeger.

Isenberg, J. P., and S. C. Rains. 1991. Peer conflict and conflict resolution among preschool children. In *The role of formal education in conflict resolution: The annual review of conflict knowledge and conflict resolution: The Role of Formal Education in Conflict Resolution,* vol. 3., edited by J. Gittler and L. Bowen. New York: Garland.

Johnson, D. W., R. T. Johnson, B. Dudley, M. Ward, and D. Magnuson. 1995. The impact of peer mediation training on the management of school and home conflicts. *American Educational Research Journal* 32, no. 4: 829–44.

Kreidler, W. J. 1990. *Elementary perspectives 1: Teaching concepts of peace and conflict.* Cambridge, Mass.: Educators for Social Responsibility.

———. 1994. *Conflict resolution in middle schools.* Cambridge, Mass.: Educators for Social Responsibility.

———. 1994. *Teaching conflict resolution through children's literature.* New York: Scholastic Professional Books.

Lappe, F. M., and P. M. DuBois. 1994. *The quickening of America: Rebuilding our nation, remaking our lives.* San Francisco: Jossey-Bass.

Lieber, C. M. 1998. *Conflict resolution in the high school.* Cambridge, Mass.: Educators for Social Responsibility.

Loeber, R., and D. P. Farrington. 1998. *Serious and violent juvenile offenders: Risk factors and successful interventions.* Thousand Oaks, Calif.: Sage.

Noddings, N. 1986. *The challenge to care in schools.* New York: Teachers College Press.

O'Toole, M. 2001. FBI Threat Assessment Report. *U.S. Federal Bureau of Investigation* at http://hamfish.org/pub/fbiss.pdf (accessed July 2, 2002).

Prothrow-Stith, D. 1991. *Deadly consequences: How violence is destroying our teenage population and a plan to begin solving the problem.* New York: Harper Perennial.

Reardon, B., and E. Nordland, eds. 1994. *Learning peace: The promise of ecological and cooperative education.* Albany: SUNY Press.

Reinhart, M. 1995. Understanding the concept of peace: A search for common ground. *Peace and Change* 20, no. 3: 379–96.

Sleeter, C. E., and C. A. Grant. 1994. *Making choices for multicultural education: Five approaches to race, class, and gender.* 2d ed. Englewood Cliffs, N.J.: Merrill/Prentice-Hall.

Stomfay-Stitz, A. M. 1993. *Peace education in America, 1928–1990: Sourcebook for education and research.* Metuchen, N.J.: Scarecrow Press.

Taylor, R. T. 2000. *Assessment of exceptional students: Educational and psychological procedures.* Boston, Mass.: Allyn and Bacon.

Tolan, P., and N. Guerra. 1994. What works in reducing adolescent violence: An empirical review of the field. Center paper for the Center for the Study and Prevention of Violence, July, at Boulder, Colo.

Walker, H. 1983. *Walker Problem Behavior Identification Checklist.* Los Angeles: Western Psychological Services.

Walker, H., and S. McConnell. 1995. *Walker-McConnell Scale of Social Competence and School Adjustment.* San Diego: Singular.

Williams, K. 1998. *Learning limits: College women, drugs, and relationships.* Westport, Conn.: Bergin and Garvey.

———. 2001. Does increasing awareness of put-downs actually reduce violence? An analysis of two rural elementary schools. Paper presented at the American Education Research Association annual meeting, April, at Seattle, Wash.

———. 2002. Determining the effectiveness of anger management training and curricular infusion at an alternative school for students expelled for weapons. *Journal of Urban Education* 37, no. 1: 59–76.

CURRICULA

Carpenter, S. 1977. *A Repertoire of Peace-Making Skills.* Consortium of Peace Research, Education and Development.

Consensus Building Institute. *Program for Young Negotiators.* Contact Person: Bruce B. Richman, Associate Director, 131 Mt. Auburn Street, Cambridge, MA 02138.

Families and Schools Together (FAST). University of Wisconsin-Madison, 1025 West Johnson Street, Madison, WI 53706; telephone: 608-263-9476, fax: 608-263-6488.

Institute for Mental Health Initiatives. 1991. *Anger Management: The RE-THINK Method.* Distributed by Research Press, 2612 N. Mattis Avenue, Champaign, IL 61821.

Kreidler, W. 1984. *Creative conflict resolution.* Glenview, Ill.: Scott Foresman.

Mundy, L., and E. Wissa. 1993. *Help increase the peace: A manual for facilitators.* American Friends Service Committee, e-mail: hippuyp@igc.apc.org

National Coalition Building Institute (NCBI). Contact person: Sherry Brown; School Change available online at www.ncbi.org.

No Putdowns Program Materials. CONTACT, Inc., (315) 251-1400 or CONTACT-Syracuse, Inc., 3049 E. Genesee St., Syracuse, NY 13244.

Prutzman, P. M., L. Burger, G. Bodenhamer, and L. Stern. 1978. *The friendly classroom for a small planet.* Wayne, N.J.: Avery.

Resolving Conflict Creatively Program. Contact information: Jennifer Selfridge, Project Director, 23 Garden Street, Cambridge, MA 02131; e-mail: jselfridge@esrnational.org. More information available online at www.esrnational.org.

Schmidt, F., and A. Friedman. 1990. *Fighting fair: Dr. Martin Luther King Jr. for kids.* Miami, Fla.: Grace Contrino Abrams Peace Education Foundation.

READINGS FROM INTERNET RESOURCES

Association for Conflict Resolution. http://www.acresolution.org/

Early Warning, Timely Response: A Guide to Safe Schools. http://www.ed.gov and http://www.air-dc.org/cecp

First Annual Report on School Safety. Office of Juvenile Justice and Delinquency Prevention. http://www.ed.gov

Hamilton Fish National Institute on School and Community Violence, with reports of promising and demonstrated practices and National School Crime and Safety Survey. www.hamfish.org

Indicators of School Crime and Safety. http://nces.ed.gov or http://www.ojp.us-doj.gov

National School Safety Center. http://www.nssc1.org

Office of Juvenile Justice and Delinquency Prevention. www.ncjrs.org/ojjdp. Participant Packet from the White House Conference on School Safety information on FAST, RCCP, PAL, and San Diego's comprehensive program

Safe and Drug-Free Schools, with several links to other resources and readings and list of exemplary practices with links to contact names. www.ed.gov/offices. OESE/SDFS

What works: Research in brief. National Institute of Justice. www.usdoj.gov

REFERENCES

Achenbach, T. M. 1991. *Teacher's Report Form*. Burlington: University of Vermont Department of Psychiatry.

Ahmad, Y., and P. K. Smith. 1994. Bullying in schools and the issue of sex differences. In *Male violence*, edited by J. Archer. London: Routledge.

American Academy of Child and Adolescent Psychiatry at www.aacap.org (accessed July 29, 2002).

Banks, R. 1997. *Bullying in schools*. ERIC Digest: ERIC Clearinghouse on Elementary and Early Childhood Education, Champaign, Ill. ERIC Number ED 407154.

Bastian, L., and B. Taylor. 1995. *School crime*. Washington, D.C.: U.S. Department of Justice, Bureau of Justice Statistics, 1991. (NCJ-131645).

Batsche, G. M., and H. M. Knoff. 1994. Bullies and their victims: Understanding a pervasive problem in the schools. *School Psychology Review* 23, no. 2: 165–74. EJ 490 574.

Brown, L., and J. Leigh. 1986. *Adaptive Behavior Inventory*. Austin, Tex.: Pro-Ed.

Burstyn, J., and R. D. Davis. 2002. The Syracuse Social, Emotional, and Academic Success Program: Its effect on students identified as violent. Paper presented at the Safe Schools for the Twenty-First Century conference, June 19–21, at Monterey, Calif.

Centers for Disease Control. 2001. Unintentional injuries, violence, and the health of young people. School Health Program Fact Sheet. *National Center for Chronic Disease Prevention and Health Promotion Adolescent and School*

Health at www.cdc.gov/nccdphp/dash/guidelines/injury_facts.htm (accessed June 12, 2002).

Charach, A., D. Pepler, and S. Ziegler. 1995. Bullying at school—A Canadian perspective: A survey of problems and suggestions for intervention. *Education Canada* 35, no. 1: 12–18. EJ 502 058.

Character Education Information. *National Center for Youth Issues* at www.charactered.net (accessed July 8, 2002).

Cornell, D. 2002. School guidelines for responding to student violence. Paper presented at the Safe Schools for the Twenty-First Century conference, June 19–21, at Monterey, Calif.

Corvo, K. N., and K. M. Williams. 2002. Substance abuse, parenting styles, and aggression: An exploratory study of weapon-carrying students. *Journal of Alcohol and Drug Education* 47, no. 3 (June).

Creating safe and drug free schools: An action guide. 1996. Washington, D.C.: Office of Juvenile Justice and Delinquency Prevention, Department of Justice.

Crowe, T. D. 1991. *Crime Prevention through Environmental Design: Applications of architectural design and space management concepts.* Stoneham, Mass.: Butterworth.

Derzon, J. H., and S. J. Wilson. 1999. An empirical review of school-based programs to reduce violence. *Hamilton Fish National Institute on School and Community Violence* at http://hamfish.org/pub/schoolint.pdf (accessed July 8, 2002).

Diagnostic and Statistical Manual of Mental Disorders: DSM-IV. 1994. 4th ed. Washington, D.C.: American Psychiatric Association.

Effective violence prevention programs. 2001. *Hamilton Fish National Institute on School and Community Violence* at http://hamfish.org/pub/evpp.html (accessed June 8, 2002).

Epp, J. R., and A. M. Watkinson. 1996. *Systemic violence: How schools hurt children.* London: Falmer Press.

Fast Response Survey: Principal/school disciplinarian survey on school violence, FRSS 63. 1997. Washington, D.C.: U.S. Department of Education, National Center for Education Statistics.

Furlong, M., and G. Morrison. 2002. In search of turning points: The future of school safety. Paper presented at the Safe Schools for the Twenty-First Century conference, June 19–21, at Monterey, Calif.

Furlong, M. J., M. P. Bates, and D. C. Smith. 2001. Predicting school weapon possession: A secondary analysis of the youth risk behavior surveillance survey. *Psychology and the School* 38, no. 2: 127–39.

Galtung, J. 1969. Violence, peace, and peace research. *Journal of Peace Research*, 167–91.

Goldstein, A. P., and E. McGinnis. 1997. *Skillstreaming the adolescent: New strategies and perspectives for teaching prosocial skills.* Champaign, Ill.: Research Press.

Hamilton Fish National Institute on School and Community Violence. 2000. *Annotated Bibliography on Alternative Education* at http://hamfish.org/pub/altedbib.html (accessed October 7, 2002).

Hawkins, D. J., R. F. Catalano, and J. Miller. 1992. Risk and Protective Factors for Alcohol and Other Drug Problems in Adolescence and Early Adulthood: Implications for Substance Abuse Prevention. *American Psychological Association Bulletin* 112: 64–105.

Hawkins, J. D., T. I. Herrenkohl, D. P. Farrington, D. Brewer, R. F. Catalano, T. W. Harachi, and L. Cothern. 2000. Predictors of youth violence. *Juvenile Justice Bulletin,* Office of Juvenile Justice and Delinquency Prevention.

Hernandez, A. 1998. *Peace in the streets: Breaking the cycle of gang violence.* Washington, D.C.: Child Welfare League of America.

Kachur, S. P. 1996. School-associated violent deaths in the United States, 1992 to 1994. *Journal of the American Medical Association* 275, no. 22 (June 12): 1729–33.

Klinefelter, A. 2002. Getting to the core of the hurt: Relational aggression amongst girls. Paper presented at the Safe Schools for the Twenty-First Century conference, June 19–21, at Monterey, Calif.

Loeber, R., and D. P. Farrington. 1998. *Serious and violent juvenile offenders: Risk factors and successful interventions.* Thousand Oaks, Calif.: Sage.

MacDonald, I. 1998. Navigating towards a safe and caring school. Paper presented at the annual meeting of the American Educational Research Association, April 13–17, at San Diego, Calif.

Mansfield, W., D. Alexander, and E. Farris. 1991. Teacher survey on safe, disciplined, and drug-free schools, Fast Response Survey System, FRSS 42. Washington, D.C.: U.S. Department of Education, National Center for Education Statistics. NCES 91-091.

Martineau, S. 1996. Dangerous liaison: The eugenics movement and the educational state. In *Systemic violence: How schools hurt children,* edited by J. R. Epp and A. M. Watkinson. Bristol, Penn.: Falmer Press.

Merriam-Webster's Collegiate Dictionary, 10th ed. s.v. "violence" at www.m-w.com/cgi-bin/dictionary?book=Dictionary&va=violence (accessed July 31, 2002).

New Collegiate Dictionary. Springfield, Mass.: G & C Merriam.

Noddings, N. 1992. *The challenge to care in schools.* New York: Teachers College Press.

Nolan, M. J., E. Daily, and K. Chandler. 1995. *Student victimization at school.* Washington, D.C.: U.S. Department of Education, National Center for Education Statistics. NCES 95-204.

———. 1995. *Student victimization at school.* Washington, D.C.: National Center for Education Statistics, Statistics in Brief, NCES 95-204. ED 388 439.

Oliver, R., J. H. Hoover, and R. Hazler. 1994. The perceived roles of bullying in small-town Midwestern schools. *Journal of Counseling and Development* 72, no. 4: 416–19. EJ 489 169.

Olweus, D. 1993. *Bullying at school: What we know and what we can do.* Cambridge, Mass.: Blackwell. ED 384 437.

Prevent Child Abuse New York. *Child Abuse Prevention Network* at http://child-abuse.com (accessed July 23, 2002).

Relationship Violence Warning Signs. *University of Buffalo Counseling Center,* 1998, at http://ub-counseling.buffalo.edu/warnings.shtml (accessed July 18, 2002).

Remboldt, C. 1994. Solving Violence Problems in Your School, *Johnson Institute/Hazelden* at www.hazelden.org/newsletter_detail.dbm?ID=804 (accessed June 8, 2002).

Revised Sexual Harassment Guidance: Harassment of Students by School Employees, Other Students, or Third Parties, Title IX. 2002. *Office of Civil Rights* at www.ed.gov/offices/OCR/shguide/index.html (accessed July 22, 2002).

Rhodes, L. K. 1992. *Literacy sssessment: A handbook of instruments.* Westport, Conn.: Heinemann.

Safe, Disciplined, and Drug Free Schools Expert Panel Report. *U.S. Department of Education* at www.ed.gov/offices/OERI/ORAD/KAD/expert_panel/drug-free.html (accessed July 10, 2002).

Schneider, T. Safer Schools through Environmental Design. *University of Oregon,* 2001, ERIC Digest 144, at http://eric.uoregon.edu/publications/digests/digest144.html (accessed July 24, 2002).

School Actions and Reactions to Discipline Issues. *U.S. Department of Education, National Center for Education Statistics*, 1998, at nces.ed.gov/pubs98/violence (accessed March 8, 2001).

School Staff Guide to Risk and Resiliency. 1997. Tallahassee, Fla.: Bureau of Instructional Support and Community Services, Division of Public Schools and Community Education, Florida Department of Education.

Sherman, L. W., D. Gottfredson, D. L. MacKenzie, J. Eck, P. Reuter, and S. D. Bushway. 1998. Preventing crime: What works, what doesn't, what's promising. Washington, D.C.: National Institute of Justice: Research in Brief, U.S. Department of Justice, Office of Justice Programs.

Sjostrom, L., and N. Stein. 1996. *Bully proof: A teacher's guide on teasing and bullying for use with fourth and fifth grade students*. Boston, Mass.: Wellesley College Center for Research on Women and the NEA Professional Library. PS 024 450.

Smith, P. K., and S. Sharp. 1994. *School Bullying: Insights and Perspectives*. London: Routledge. ED 387 223.

Sprague, J., G. Colvin, and L. Irvin. 1995. *The Oregon school safety survey*. Eugene: University of Oregon Press.

Strengthening Families. *Iowa State University Extension* at www.extension.iastate.edu/sfp (accessed July 28, 2002).

Taylor, R. T. 2000. *Assessment of exceptional students: Educational and psychological procedures*. Boston, Mass.: Allyn and Bacon.

Tjaden, P., and N. Thoennes. 1998. Prevalence, incidents, and consequences of violence against women: Findings from the national violence against women survey. *National Institute of Justice Centers for Disease Control and Prevention: Research in Brief* at http://ncjrs.org/pdffiles/172837.pdf (accessed July 8, 2002).

Tolan, P., and N. Guerra. 1994. What works in reducing adolescent violence: An empirical review of the field. Paper presented at the Study and Prevention of Violence, University of Colorado, Boulder.

Walker, H. 1983. *Walker Problem Behavior Identification Checklist*. Los Angeles: Western Psychological Services.

———. 1995. The acting-out child: Coping with classroom disruption. Longmont, Colo.: Sopris West.

Walker, H., G. Colvin, and E. Ramsey. 1995. *Antisocial behavior in school strategies and best practices*. Pacific Grove, Calif.: Wadsworth.

Walker, H., and S. McConnell. 1995. *Walker-McConnell Scale of Social Competence and School Adjustment*. San Diego: Singular.

Warning signs: Recognizing signs of violence in others. *American Psychological Association* at http://helping.apa.org/warningsigns/recognizing.html (accessed July 25, 2002).

Whitney, I., and P. K. Smith. 1993. A survey of the nature and extent of bullying in junior/middle and secondary schools. *Educational Research* 35, no. 1: 3–25. EJ 460 708.

Williams, K. M. 1998. *Learning limits: College women, drugs, and relationships*. Westport, Conn.: Bergin and Garvey.

———. 2001. Does increasing awareness of put-downs actually reduce violence? An analysis of two rural elementary schools. Paper presented at the American Education Research Association annual meeting in Seattle, Washington.

Wolowiec, J., ed. 1994. *Everybody wins: Mediation in the schools*. Chicago: American Bar Association.

INDEX

ABOUT THE AUTHOR

Dr. Kimberly M. Williams is a faculty member for the State University of New York at Cortland's School of Education. She coordinates the evaluation for the Safe Schools, Healthy Students project for the Syracuse City School District, and previously coordinated Syracuse University's subcontract of the Hamilton Fish National Institute on School and Community Violence.

Most recently, Dr. Williams authored the book *Learning Limits: College Women, Drugs, and Relationships*, chapters in *Preventing Violence in Schools: A Challenge to American Democracy*, and articles on school violence for the *Journal of Urban Education*, the *Journal of Drug Education*, and the *American School Board Journal*. Dr. Williams continues her research on violence prevention, gives presentations and workshops on school violence prevention and intervention strategies, and teaches courses on research methods and assessment to preservice and in-service teachers and administrators.